Rebound 1970

This book may be kept

The Genius of

S P A I N

and other Essays

On Spanish Contemporary Literature

The Genius of

SPAIN

and other essays on

Spanish Contemporary

Literature

by

SALVADOR DE MADARIAGA

Author of *Shelley and Calderon and other essays
on English and Spanish Poetry*

OXFORD 3-075-6
AT THE CLARENDON PRESS
1923

Oxford University Press

London   Edinburgh   Glasgow   Copenhagen
New York   Toronto   Melbourne   Cape Town
Bombay   Calcutta   Madras   Shanghai
Humphrey Milford Publisher to the UNIVERSITY

Printed in England

PREFACE

THERE was a time—not long ago—when Spanish fiction was scantily though honourably represented in English-speaking countries by *Pepita Jiménez*. It is now nearly omnipresent owing to the novels of Blasco Ibañez. In either case, the English reader could hardly be expected to form a clear idea of Spanish letters from the knowledge of one single type of mind, be it fastidiously aristocratic as that of Don Juan Valera, or exuberantly popular as that of the vigorous author of *The Four Horsemen of the Apocalypse*.

The essays collected in this volume aim at a wider and more comprehensive view of the field of Spanish contemporary literature. In harmony with one of the most typical features of the Spanish character as here analysed, this study has been cast in the form of literary portraits of living authors. These include most of the prominent figures of the group known in Spain as the 1898 generation. Students of Spanish letters will, however, miss a few familiar names belonging to this group, such as Ramiro de Maeztu, a mind sadly dispersed, though by no means lost, in journalistic work, and Ortega y Gasset, whose bent is too philosophical for our present purpose. These omissions are compensated for by the inclusion of two men from outside the 1898 group—Pérez de Ayala and Gabriel Miró.

An introduction has been found necessary, not only

as a background for these figures, but also in order that they might be seen in relation to the spirit of the country and of Europe in general. An essay on Galdós and a note on Don Francisco Giner have been added to this introduction in view of the prominent rôle which the great novelist and his contemporary played in the formation of the present generation. A third article on Menéndez y Pelayo would have been inserted here had not the author felt unable to cope with the task of drawing a sketch, however slight, of so powerful and so widely developed an intellect.

The essays are published in the order in which they were written. It remains to be said that most of them have seen the light in diverse reviews. The second part of the introductory essay, in the *London Mercury*; the essay on Galdós in the *Contemporary Review*; that on Unamuno, as an introduction to the admirable translation of *The Tragic Sense of Life* which we owe to the pen of Mr. Crawford Flitch, and for the publication of which Messrs. Macmillan deserve the thanks of all English lovers of Spanish literature; the essay on Baroja appeared in French in *La Revue de Genève*; and those on Valle Inclán and on Azorin and Miró in *Hermes*, the brilliant review of which Bilbao was proud until a recent date and which we hope will see the light again.

S. DE M.

CONTENTS

INTRODUCTION

I. THE GENIUS OF SPAIN

THE political decadence of what once was the greatest Empire of modern times has led uninformed people to underestimate, and even to neglect altogether, one of the richest amongst those national essences the synthesis of which we call European genius. Yet the Spanish language should be a sufficient sign of its importance. 'Le style, c'est l'homme,' said Buffon. He might just as aptly have said : *The language is the nation.* But here a word of caution may be permitted. A language is not a mere mob of words drilled into logical order by means of a grammar. It is a living natural phenomenon the evolution of which is determined by the action of inner or psychological forces on outer or philological matter. For our present purpose, therefore, what is important in a language is its soul, not its body. Hence the classification of peoples according to the philological origin of the language they speak cannot but be misleading. It rests on the assumption that community of origin is more important than the differences evolved in centuries of use ; whereas the first is a purely accidental phenomenon (generally due to common conquest by a more civilized people) while the latter are essential, and flow from differences in national character. It is obvious that a red-haired citizen of Aberdeen and a negro from Richmond (Virginia) have but little in common, though they both speak languages which can be traced back to Chaucer. Similarly, though less obviously, the fact that the

6 8/1

French and the Spaniards have evolved from the same
Latin stock two tongues so different in music and in
spirit, is sufficient to dispose of the legend of ' The
Latin Peoples ' in so far as this name is meant to
suggest a similarity in nature and character between
the Romance-speaking nations. The point is the more
important for the subtle association of ideas which
connects the word ' Latin ' with the classics and
antiquity. Now, though there is much to be said for
an interpretation of French character and culture as
a more or less direct descendant of Athenian wisdom
and intellectual acumen, and though Italy may be said
to be closely related to Greek ideals of life, nothing in
Europe is farther removed from the Spanish genius than
the genius of Greece. Certain Roman traits, stoicism,
pomp, there are in the Spanish character. But if Latin
is to mean classical polish and culture there are few
countries in Europe more un-' Latin ' than Spain.[1]

Spanish, though Latin in body, is in spirit a language instinct with a genius of its own, thoroughly
different, not only from French and Italian, but from
that vague ethnical entity which goes by the name of
Latinity. Forget for one moment its unfortunate
commercial preponderance. Divest your mind from
the pitiless statistics which prove its dominions to be
second in area and third in population among those
of the other languages of Europe, and think of it purely
as an instrument for the expression of man. Where
among living tongues is there one more beautiful ?

Its range of musical possibilities is wider than that

---

[1] History confirms this purely critical observation. Thus, Professor
Altamira remarks that the civilization of modern Spain began in
Galicia, Asturias, León, and Castile, that is in the least Romanized
parts of the Peninsula, while the east and south, regions where the
influence of Rome had been greatest, remained under Moorish sway
(*Historia de España y de la Civilización Española*, vol. ii, p. 239,
ed. 1913).

of French, German, or Italian, and at least equal to
that of English. Over Italian it has the superiority
of its stronger framework and its more clear-cut
architecture. German is a powerful organ and French
an exquisite violin. But each has the limitations of its
powers. Even if the German language can render such
tuneful moanings as :

> Les sanglots longs
> Des violons
> De l'automne . . .,

it can hardly attain the frail delicacy of airs such as :

> Un petit roseau m'a suffi
> Pour faire frémir l'herbe haute
> Et tout le pré,
> Et les doux saules,
> Et le ruisseau qui chante aussi.
> Un petit roseau m'a suffi
> A faire frémir la forêt. . . .

The French language, on the other hand, has not
enough volume of voice to fill out with sound sentences
such as :

> In eurem Namen, Mutter, die ihr thront
> Im Gränzenlosen, ewig einsam wohnt
> Und doch gesellig. *Faust*, ii. 6427,

still less to achieve that musical plenitude which Milton
attains in one line :

> Thrones, Dominations, Princedoms, Virtues, Powers !
> *Paradise Lost*, x. 459.

English can be light and airy, and in its best Elizabethan form has a spontaneous charm which is to the
grace of French poetry what fresh-gathered violets are
to perfume of exquisite manufacture. Usually, however, it is only under the weight of thought that it
softens its somewhat jerky monosyllabic stride, and it
does not seem to be able to glide peacefully along in
dreamy passivity.

Spanish can cover all these styles. It can sail majestically over seas of Miltonian eloquence :

> Voz de dolor y canto de gemido
> Y espíritu de miedo envuelto en ira,
> Hagan principio acerbo a la memoria
> De aquel día fatal, aborrecido,
> Que Lusitania mísera suspira,
> Desnuda de valor, falta de gloria. . . .
>
> F. de Herrera ;

it can vie in musical plenitude with the organ-like cadences of German :

> De la viva y creciente incertidumbre
> Que en lucha estéril nuestra fuerza agota ;
> Del huracán de sangre que alborota
> El mar de la revuelta muchedumbre ;
> De la insaciable y honda podredumbre
> Que el rostro y la conciencia nos azota.
>
> G. Nuñez de Arce.

But those are its best-known virtues. Not so widely recognized is its sprightly grace for dancing tunes, witness this delightful quatrain of that exquisite musician, Don Ramón del Valle Inclán :

> Como en la gaita del galáico
> Pastor, de la orilla del Miño,
> Salte la gracia del trocáico
> Verso, ligero como un niño.
>
> *La Marquesa Rosalinda*, Preludio.

or the Verlainian sonority which it can yield under an emotional strain ; thus, Rubén Darío :

> Juventud, divino tesoro,
> Ya te vas para no volver.
> Cuando quiero llorar, no lloro,
> Y a veces lloro sin querer.

Its energy is proverbial and in its assertive octosyllabic it possesses an unrivalled instrument for the expression of manly strength or for the rendering of pithy proverb-like sentences. It is well known that

Corneille frequently endeavoured to imitate the sudden discharges of energy of our dramatic octosyllabic. But Racine, though a genius of so different a type and so much less dependent on stage effect, does not seem averse from seeking in Spain the model for some of his neatest and most telling phrases. Thus, his famous

Trop pour la concubine et trop peu pour l'épouse

seems to me to be directly imitated from Alarcón, in *Las Paredes oyen*:

> Grande para dama soy
> Si pequeña para esposa.
>
> Act III, Sc. ii.

Energy, again, is a quality too well known in the Spanish language, and by insisting on it we may be led to overlook how tender this language can be with St. John of the Cross; how classically elegant with Fray Luis de León; how peasant-like in its fervid simplicity with St. Teresa; how refined and courtly with Garcilaso; how eloquent with Herrera; how direct and effective with Lope; how moving in some lyrical sonnets of Quevedo, and how complex, resourceful, and adaptable in the moderns. Yet, all these qualities are not equally inherent in its nature; and as the most typical of the Spanish language and character, even above its energy, I would select a rare power, difficult to define, a kind of genius for direct utterance which enables it to attain great emotional or spiritual effects by means of daily, humble words, expressive of daily, humble ideas, precisely that poetic quality—it will be recognized—which Wordsworth strove all his life to acquire. Thus, in Bécquer:

> Cerraron sus ojos
> Que aun tenía abiertos;
> Taparon su cara
> Con un blanco lienzo;

Y unos sollozando,
Otros en silencio,
De la triste alcoba
Todos se salieron.

A language which can be at the same time so bare
and so beautiful is the creation of a great national
spirit. And thus, even if no other facts were available,
a study of Spanish poetry would be sufficient to establish that though Spain may not be in the front rank
of political and economic powers, she undoubtedly is
one of the great spiritual powers of the world.

But in order to give a measure of this greatness, we
may look back upon certain historical facts, mere
indices of quantity which may serve to fix the scale
of Spain's contribution to the spiritual life of Europe.
Thus, if we consider the history of Europe's great
achievements, we find Spain the protagonist of the
most important event in the life of the human race
since the fall of the Roman Empire. The discovery
of America was not a mere lucky prize which Fate let
fall on the lap of Spain. It was above all a masterpiece
of faith and creative imagination. Moreover, it
opened an era of Spanish travel and discovery which,
taken as a whole, constitutes perhaps the greatest epic
which the human race has known. Lapses of cupidity
and fits of cruelty there were in it. But particularly
when reduced from legendary exaggerations to their
real historical dimensions and seen in their true
perspective, in relation to the whole attitude of Spanish
conquerors and to that of other colonizing races, they
do not suffice to abate the splendour of the discovery
and conquest of America. Such deeds as Cortés
burning his ships, or Balboa kneeling

Silent, upon a peak in Darien,

in sight of the new discovered Pacific are still awaiting
a Homer worthy of them.

If from history we turn to literature we shall find the genius of Spain no less great and original. Spain can boast of that unique creation, the *Romancero*, less an epic poem than an epic growth, which, born almost wild all over her land and preserved by verbal tradition in the memory of her people, has since acquired universal celebrity, and given the seed of inspiration to Heine and Victor Hugo, Southey, Byron, and Walter Scott.

Spain shares with England the rare distinction of having originated a national theatre. The Golden Century is one of the few great literary epochs of the world, comparable to the Elizabethan era and to the ' Siècle de Louis XIV '. Though rich in novels and lyrical poetry and essays and every kind of literary production, the Golden Century is above all celebrated for the incomparable splendour of its theatre.

If the six greatest names of European literature be singled out, it is likely that the choice of them would be somewhat as follows : Shakespeare, Cervantes, Dante, Goethe, Rabelais, and Tolstoy. There might be discussions as to this or that name, but if there are two which are safe on the list, they certainly are those of the Englishman and the Spaniard.

As with authors, so with books. Who would doubt that the greatest book written in any European language is *Don Quixote* ; this novel, the first in date and the first in excellence, from which all other novels in more than one sense *descend* ?

And if we are to judge nations by their power to create characters—those characters of art which live a life much richer, fuller, and longer than the characters of nature—here again Spain will hold her own in the first rank. Let the four greatest characters of European literature be named. Hamlet and Faust will be of the number ; the other two will have to come from Spain : Don Quixote and Don Juan, and they are

the greatest of the four. Hamlet is too much of a
dream and Faust too much of an idea. But Don
Quixote and Don Juan are men of flesh and blood,
of our own flesh and blood, and they will live and grow
as long as men are moved by love of justice or love
of woman.

Thus, a brief series of rough valuations shows Spain
to be in the front line of European powers when
judged by spiritual standards. Each of these powers
brings to the European genius a contribution of its
own, a complex national spirit which is difficult to
define yet can be briefly suggested. Bar England,
and Europe loses that sense of harmony between
ethical Heaven and positive Earth which is to the
progress of mankind what the instinctive alliance of
eyes and feet is to man's walk. Bar France, and
Europe is the poorer for the geometric spirit which
in the confusion of nature's forms can detect the
immovable lines of principles. Bar Italy and the
sense of polished culture and intellectual enjoyment
of life disappears from the European world. Bar
Germany, and Europe is left without her central
laboratory and storehouse where all her thoughts are
received, compared, tested, and developed and made
into one. Bar Russia, and the stem which unites the
European branch to its Asiatic root is cut off. Bar
Spain, and what will be the loss to Europe ?

We may approach the definition of it by a negative
remark. The contribution of Spain to Europe is
least important in the region of principles and theory.
True, the scientific work of Spain is generally under-
estimated, and in this as in many other subjects
a thorough revision of prevalent ideas must sometime
be undertaken. But it is, I believe, possible to set
down two observations on the matter. The first,
that the scientific work of Spain has always been and

still is most prominent in applied science; that though Spain has given to the world many a philosophic and scientific minor genius, she cannot be said without obvious exaggeration to have given birth to a single genius of the first magnitude in either science or philosophy. Men of the intellectual eminence of Newton or Pascal, Descartes, Kant, or Poincaré, there never were south of the Pyrenees. Still less can we speak of any great school of scientific or philosophic thought having taken birth or brilliant development within the cultural boundaries of Spain; for not only were the intellectual leaders lacking, but the tendency towards extreme individualism to be observed in Spanish thought no less than in Spanish life always worked against the fusion of individual opinions into collective systems or movements. So that on the whole it may not unfairly be said that, much as applied sciences, such as geography, natural history, and jurisprudence, owe to Spain, the contribution of Spain to the spirit of Europe is least important in the region of abstract thought.

We are thus confronted with the first feature of Spanish thought. It is concrete and it is applied. It shuns abstraction. Pure speculation is not to its taste and it abhors byzantinism. In this respect there is a close likeness between the Spanish and the English character, since both find in practice and action their most congenial task. Yet there is an all-important difference. Direct observation will show that the ideal of the Englishman is ethical, social, and positive; that of the Spaniard is æsthetical, individual, and personal. The Englishman's norm is virtue, the Spaniard's norm is honour; the Englishman seeks action in order to conquer things; the Spaniard in order to conquer men. For the main interest of the Spaniard is in man.

But we must define this word, MAN, which is too

frequently used to be equally understood by every one. And I feel that I could give no better definition of the meaning which it has for Spain than the opening words of Miguel de Unamuno's masterpiece, *El Sentimiento Trágico de la Vida*.[1] The first chapter of this book under the title of ' The Man of Flesh and Bones ', begins with the following words :

> *Homo sum ; nihil humani a me alienum puto,* said the Latin playwright. And I would rather say, *nullum hominem a me alienum puto* ; I am a man, no other man do I deem a stranger. For the adjective *humanus* is as suspect to me as its abstract substantive *humanitas,* humanity. Neither the human nor humanity, neither the simple nor the sub-stantivized adjective, but the concrete substantive, *man.* The man of flesh and bones, he who is born, suffers and dies—particularly, dies—he who eats and drinks and plays and sleeps and thinks and wills, the man who sees and is heard, the brother, the true brother.
>
> For there is another thing, which they also call man, and which is the subject of not a few divagations more or less scientific. And it is the featherless biped of the legend, the ζῷον πολιτικόν of Aristotle, the social contracting party of Rousseau, the *homo oeconomicus* of the Manchesterians, the *homo sapiens* of Linnæus, or if so preferred, the vertical mammal. A man who is neither here nor there, who belongs neither to this nor to that epoch, who has neither sex nor country, in one word, an idea. That is, a not-man.

Thus, in what he is and in what he is not, Unamuno admirably defines the man of Spanish philosophy of life, the man of flesh and bones. It is this man who is the main if not the only subject of Spanish art and literature. No other nation—save perhaps Shakespeare, a nation unto himself—can show such a strong tendency towards the creation of concrete types of human beings. Observe how, all through Spanish art, definite types, on canvas, in the novel, or in

[1] An English translation of this work is now available, *The Tragic Sense of Life in Men and Peoples*, Macmillan & Co., 1921.

drama, stand out in such relief that in contrast the
background of nature and circumstance sinks into
insignificance. From the very outset Spanish literature centres on the doings of that great man, El Cid.
The Archpriest of Hita is so richly endowed with the
creative gift that, not content with founding in
Trotaconventos, that great though disreputable dynasty
to which later on Celestina was to give eternal lustre,
he can transform into living beings pagan myths such
as Doña Venus and Don Amor, as well as Christian
abstractions such as Doña Cuaresma and Don Carnal.
La Celestina is a marvellous set of characters created
in true dramatic fashion out of the very stuff of action.
It is unnecessary to dwell on the picaresque novels,
still less on *Don Quixote*, the two prominent heroes of
which tend to overshadow the multitude of other
persons who throng its lively pages. The Spanish
Theatre, it is true, created a relatively small number
of characters. But this fact is perhaps due to an excess
rather than to a defect of creative power. That the
power was there is shown by such figures as Pedro
Crespo (*El Alcalde de Zalamea*), Segismundo (*La
Vida es sueño*), Enrico (*El Condenado por Desconfiado*),
many of Tirso's women and above all Don Juan.
But the Spanish Theatre had to satisfy the truly
Gargantuan appetite of the public for plays, and the
result was that dramatists wrote in great haste, as it
were while the public and the actors waited. Full
development of characters was impossible under such
conditions. Moreover, most of their plays should be
considered as mere sketches and exercises in character
rather than as attempts at complete creation. The
taste of the public for human life, that is for men in
action, required an ever renewed supply of plots and
situations which it was not thought worth while
developing, suggestion being sufficient for a society
highly trained in dramatic pleasure. For our present

purpose it is, however, enough to point out that the Spanish Theatre constitutes an immense quarry of character-material, more or less elaborated at the hands of ever-hurried dramatists.

Nor need we limit our remarks to literature. What is Spanish painting but a unique gallery of portraits ? A monk by Zurbarán, a prince, a buffoon, a pagan god, a Christ, by Velázquez, an apostle, a magdalen by Ribera, a saint, a gentleman, a priest by El Greco, a lady, a general by Goya, what is it in them which, different in style as they are, makes them all members of the same family ? It is that beneath the different garbs of age and state, they all are definite men and women. Compare the Cid of Guillén de Castro to the Cid of Corneille, and you will perceive the difference between a man who is above all himself and, to use a significant Spanish saying, ' as God made him ', and on the other hand a hero endeavouring to live up to the theoretical standard of his class. Compare the Charles IV of Goya to the Louis XIV of Largillière (a comparison in which the balance of artistic merit is reversed) and you reach the same conclusion ; the one is a man who happens to be a king ; the other is a king, every inch a king, and not in the least a man. The French have endeavoured to see the type through the man ; the Spaniards have tried to give us the man beneath the type. Thus the dominant feature of Spanish art is that it is not conceived from an artistic but from a vital point of view. The Spanish artist makes art the instrument of life and not life the raw matter of art. That is why he relies less on composition, style, relations to culture or intellectual associations, than on the direct appeal to the human heart of the public from the human heart of the subject. His aim is, therefore, that which is the supreme test of all art—the fixing and recreating of life.

Such an achievement requires a creative imagination singularly free. So often and so forcibly has political Spain stood for the limitation of the freedom of thought that to speak of liberty in connexion with the spirit of Spain may seem to the uninformed paradoxical if not altogether absurd. A discussion of Spanish limitations to free thought in relation to the standards of the age, and a parallel between Philip II, Calvin, and John Knox, to mention only three prominent Definers of Faith of the period, in their respective attitudes with regard to free thinking, would take us too far away from our subject. The fact remains that few nations can vie with Spain in freedom of creative imagination, that is, in liberty from those intellectual, moral, and even æsthetical prejudices which hinder man's vision and interpretation of nature. True, it sometimes happens that a great Spanish creator sets to work with an avowed moral or intellectual purpose; it may be to show up vice in all its hatefulness and to present virtue in all its desirability to the hardened hearts of his readers—thus, Juan Ruiz and most of the authors of the picaresque novels; it may be to stamp out the pest of chivalry books—thus, Cervantes; it may be to prove a particular proposition with regard to faith and dogma, so Tirso or Calderón. But, with the exception perhaps of Calderón, whose work is too often fettered by his didactic proclivities, and still more by the tenets of a dogma too rigidly held and defined, it is curious how little all these distracting intentions and purposes seem to encumber the truly creative work of our artists. With some of them—and I would mention here the picaresque authors and the Archpriest of Hita—this is due to the fact that their moral protestations are mere pretence and a concession to the ecclesiastical authorities; with others, as for instance, Cervantes, to the sheer strength of their creative instinct. The results are

somewhat puzzling for the uninitiated. A set of bookish
ideas of a rhetorical character more or less directly
inherited from the classics, and in later years the
restraining influence of the Inquisition on moral and
intellectual issues, weave a kind of veil which spreads
over the whole of Spanish art until relatively recent
times. Yet, behind that veil, how freely conceived
and how boldly expressed are characters and ideas!
And how truly, above all other aims more or less
sincerely professed, the Spanish creative instinct
pursues that freest and highest form of beauty which
goes by the name of *character*!

A thing of beauty is a joy for ever

Keats once said. The young English poet did not live
beyond the age which loves general statements, and he
set one of them, perhaps a little flatly expressed and even
conceived, at the end of one of his most beautiful poems:

Beauty is truth, truth beauty—that is all
Ye know on earth and all ye need to know.

Well. That is as it may be. But it is best for an artist
qua artist not to know and not to inquire. When he
sets out to feel it is best that he should forget that
there is such a thing as truth or beauty, and whether
they are the same, or opposite, or merely different.
And it is well also that he should not limit his sensations even by means of such an earnest, if pleasurable,
norm of selection as joy. For in such a limitation there
is the risk of discriminating in life between things
which have and things which have not the right to be
interpreted by art, or in other words, a risk of reducing
the true and deep meaning of beauty, making of it
something akin to prettiness. Beauty is the æsthetic
radiance of life, and all that lives, if seen with the
innocent eyes of the artist, is beautiful. Thus understood, beauty coincides with the idea expressed in the
modern abstract use of the word *character*. And in

this task, the true task of all art, Spanish imagination allows no fetters.

It should, however, be noticed that such extreme liberty in the handling of reality does not imply cynicism. Montesquieu said that ' hypocrisy is the homage which vice pays to virtue', and the same might be said, though more subtly, of cynicism, since the deliberate breach no less than the feigned observance is a recognition of the law. But in its creative capacity, the Spanish genius ignores virtue altogether and neither laments its absence not exults at it. It seems to work on the assumption that, though to the ethical faculty virtue as a norm is higher and purer than life, to the æsthetical faculty it is but part of life, smaller than the whole and not entitled to any special treatment or consideration. The result strikes at once the student of Spanish art and literature. No one can read Fielding without noticing that he prefers Tom Jones to Master Blifil. Dickens himself, whose heart was great, did not take kindly to Uriah Heep and frankly disliked old Nickleby. But to the author of *La Celestina* the old procuress is as dear as love-infatuated Calixto or sweet Melibea. For, in the pregnant Spanish phrase, ' they all are sons of God '. And this truly religious impartiality inspires all great works of Spanish art and literature. It shines in every page of *Don Quixote*; it inspires every picture of Velázquez; it guides the brush of Goya and the pen of Galdós. It is the feeling which makes Spanish art and literature as impressive as a spectacle of nature—for it is indeed nature since it is created in liberty and love.

In thus making man—the complete man of flesh and bones—the main subject of her art and thoughts, Spain runs counter to the predominant tendency of Europe. Under the austere discipline of reason, Europe endeavours to repress in man all that is not

easily amenable to rule and measure. This severe
self-sacrifice is the guarantee of all philosophic and
scientific progress, of all abstract thought, in fact.
But it goes without saying that the tendency is previous
to, and more general than, purely scientific and philosophical ambitions. It is in fact a natural tendency
in the central-European type, whether under its
French, German, or Italian variety. The characteristic
faculty of continental Europe is its power for abstract
thought. Hence its art and literature. Dante,
Goethe, Rabelais, are guided in their art by definite
philosophies. Europe is objective and forces man to
stand aside in order that the mind may understand.
England, on the other hand, eminently active, seeks
above all the adjustment of the individual to a social
system so that co-operation may be most efficient and
smooth. English art, therefore, develops under a
moral-social influence. Spain, meanwhile, keeps intact
her respect for all-round man. Neither the mind, as
in Europe, nor the community, as in England, but
man himself is the point of departure of her philosophy
and of her art. Her genius is homocentric.

That is the cause of her weakness and of her strength.
Measured in area the Spanish genius is poor. Measured
in depth, it is rich. It neglects the developments which
an ever curious intellect opens out continually before
the French, the Germans, the Italians—those experi-
ments in form or in sensation to which the art of Europe
owes so much of its appeal. It does not pursue those
applications of art and thought to the business of life
which give so much weight and value to English literature. It does not disperse itself in a nice analysis of the
thousand little forces which converge upon and radiate
from a civilized citizen, but rather considers man as
a whole, in his struggle and dealings with the great
elementary powers : Evil, Death, Love.

Evil, Death, Love, are the threads of the canvas of

Time. All the rest is embroidery on the canvas. Evil (or Experience), Death, and Love are the Muses of Spanish literature. In its great lines, therefore, Spanish literature might be considered as composed of three symbolical books—a Book of Proverbs, an Ecclesiastes, and a Song of Songs.

Every one has read *Don Quixote*. Every one is familiar with the inexhaustible fund of proverbs which Sancho deals out with a generosity in him altogether exceptional. It would be a mistake to pass over that wealth of proverbs as if it were a mere ' side-show ' in the book. Far from it, it is one of its main features ; one which contributes as much as any other towards giving *Don Quixote* its representative value as the Book of Spain *par excellence*. Proverbs, indeed, are the salt not only of *Don Quixote*, but also of almost every classical Spanish narrative. They are equally conspicuous in the theatre. Not only do they occur in the text of many plays—fitting as they do into the octosyllabic scheme of versification as to the manner born—but they may be said to form the substance as they provide the title of numerous *comedias*. It is indeed hardly an exaggeration to say that many a *comedia* is but the development and the illustration of a proverb. Inversely, we must look upon most of these Spanish proverbs as real little poems, which being of a marked dramatic character, may be considered as *lightning comedias*—the last stage of a process of dramatic condensation the successive phases of which would be the *comedia*, the *entremés*, the *romance*, the popular song and the proverb. Needless to say, this succession is not suggested as historical, nor do I mean to imply that the Spanish mind passes from one to the other of these forms ; but merely to point out the existence of five different states of condensation in which dramatic matter can be found in Spanish life and literature.

The important point is that, more often than not, the proverb is of an essentially dramatic character. It may be considered as a drop of that wisdom distilled by experience, which is so typical of Spanish letters. It symbolizes one of the three main moods of the Spanish spirit—that in which the mind remains unruffled in the contemplation of men as they are, and therefore, able to see and understand man in his entirety without explaining away—still less suppressing or ignoring—awkward facts. It is in this serene mood that most of the dramatic, epic, and narrative literature, as well as a whole branch of the art of Spain is conceived ; that part of Spanish literature and art which has been here symbolized as a Book of Proverbs.

But Spain has also contributed to the living Bible of Europe a splendid Ecclesiastes. It is a much thinner book, for, on the face of it, the thought that all is vanity of vanities is enough to paralyse the pen— unless indeed the pen be driven by the desire to abolish or give relief to the thought itself. I have said that the Spanish mind was homocentric. It is, therefore, consistent in its preoccupation with death, for if it sees man as the king of creation, perforce death must acquire in its eyes the importance of a crime of *lèse-majesté*. Man is a king dethroned by death. Spain would not be true to her individualistic faith if she accepted for the solution of the puzzle of life the survival of man in his species or in his works. The race, posterity,—abstractions. The only concrete and living thing is the individual. It is the individual who is king of the world, and it is he whom death dethrones. The spirit of Spain is dominated by this idea, the shadow of its light, the reaction of its activity. Her intense feeling for life recoils upon her spirit as an equally intense feeling for death. Like those anchorites whom her painters loved to paint, she contemplates the Light of Life with the skull and cross-bones at her elbow. This mood of her creative spirit manifests itself throughout all her literature and art. Towards the close of the Middle Ages, it inspires what is perhaps the most celebrated page of the Spanish Ecclesiastes—the famous *coplas* of Jorge Manrique on the death of his father:

> Recuerde el alma dormida,
> Avive el seso y despierte,
> Contemplando,
> Cómo se pasa la vida,
> Cómo se viene la muerte,
> Tan callando. . . .

The theme is here handled with that perfect simplicity which is the secret of great masterpieces. It had been for long a favourite subject for Spanish poets, and Gómez Manrique, uncle of Jorge and in the bulk of his work a poet of greater merit, had given almost as good a version of it as that which soon afterwards became its final form. The *coplas* of Jorge Manrique became the models for generations to come. They were the subject of numberless imitations and *glosas*, both in verse and in prose, which show that the poet had stirred a sensitive string in the national soul. The theme never disappears from Spanish literature. In lyrical poetry it can be traced to this day, through some of the sombre and most poetic sonnets of Quevedo, for instance, the sonnet which begins—

> Miré los muros de la patria mía . . .

to poems published but yesterday, such as ' El Pasajero ' by Valle Inclán. There is an echo of Jorge Manrique in the beautiful stanzas of ' La Rosa de Job ':

> ¡ La vida ! . . . Polvo en el viento
> Volador.
> ¡ Sólo no muda el cimiento
> Del dolor !

In prose, the thought of death is of course one of the mainsprings of Spanish religious literature, and in modern times it inspires almost to the point of obsession the powerful genius of Don Miguel de Unamuno.

But the influence of the thought of death is not limited to religious works and lyrical poetry. It creates a mood which, though in different degrees, affects the whole of the arts and letters of Spain, and it accounts perhaps for that curious sense of detachment which most of her artists and writers convey.

Yet, though imbued with the negative spirit of Ecclesiastes, the Spanish mind does not surrender itself to Death. Far from it. There are in the depths of the Spanish soul treasures of energy sufficient to conquer spiritual pain and to triumph over the most human of infirmities. It is from this deep source of life that mysticism flows.

In her mystic or triumphant mood, Spain is no less faithful to her homocentric nature than when she dwells on the evil of life or on death. What is typical of the Spanish mystics is precisely the vital and human character of their beliefs, as opposed to the philosophical or theoretical doctrines of the mystics of other nations. Our mystics seek the survival of the individual in their union with God. St. John of the Cross, in his most celebrated poem, expresses it in clear words :

> Mira que la dolencia
> De amor, que no se cura
> Sino con la presencia y la figura.[1]

Here is love in the concrete. None of those abstractions which subtilize the most individual of all passions

---

[1] Lope de Vega is even more forcible in the following lines :
No venga ángel ni legado.
Cristo en carne evangelice :
Descienda Dios humanado.
Auto Sacramental de los Cantares.

into a kind of metaphysical category, but a concrete relation between two living beings, the creature and the Creator, the temporal and the Eternal.

It is this vital and human character which the spirit of love retains in Spanish literature even when shorn of its mystical attributes. A certain dryness and indifference to pain, a certain tendency to stiffen against tenderness, may have contributed to obscure the real love that animates it. With all its hardness, however, Spanish literature is most deeply imbued with the spirit of fraternity. Without that all-pervading feeling which unites all men in the common category of *sons of God*, the penetration revealed by such works as *La Celestina* and *Don Quixote* would have been unthinkable. Without the warmth which that feeling rouses in our soul, the sympathetic presentation of the types and characters which live in the Spanish novel would not have been even attempted. Love is the key to the understanding of such dissimilar artists as Fray Luis de León and Galdós. Of the three Muses of Spanish literature it is Death which limits the scope of subjects; it is Evil, or if you prefer, Life, which dictates the form; but it is Love which provides the main inspiration.

I have thus tried to explain the three phases of the spirit of Spain—its strophe, its antistrophe, and its catastrophe. Experience ending in disillusionment, disillusionment overcome by love. Three phases which may be summed up in one : Man complete and concrete. In the European family, therefore, Spain represents a spirit which in the face of abstractions asserts the wholeness of man; to the ' ought-to-be ' and to the ' seems-to-be ' it opposes a plain *is*. In its concreteness and all-round individualism it finds its safest guide. Abstract thought may go astray and fly too high in the clouds of pride or welter too low in the mud of cynicism. But to Spain we can always

go with confidence. She can descend to the lower
levels of life, but takes with her man's divine soul;
she can rise to mystic heights, but does not leave behind
man's earthly body. To humanity she opposes man;
to art, life; to science, passion. Shelley divined the
nature of her spirit with marvellous intuition when
he spoke of her as ' flame-like Spain '.

II. THE CHARACTER OF SPANISH
CONTEMPORARY LITERATURE

THE first impression produced on the mind by
a general survey of Spanish contemporary literature
is one of incoherence and dispersion. We miss that
social, almost official, orderliness of English literary
life, a society in itself, admirably organized with its
standards of taste, language, manners, and conduct;
with its sure instinct for placing every one of its
members in his own class, rank, function; with its
common purpose and aim, towards the fulfilment of
which all its members, whether creative, critical,
or passive, co-operate. Nor do we find in Spain those
powerful currents of literary activity which periodically
sweep over France—movements of a mind ever awake
and self-observant, generally born in some small
cénacle or chapelle, which soon grow into a legion of
keen intellectual fighters animated with all the bellicose
spirit of the Gallic race. Neither the Saxon spirit
of co-operation, nor the Gallic spirit of revolution is
available to unite and herd together Spanish creative
minds. Like the goats of the bare hills of Castile,
they seem to prefer solitary haunts among the peaks of
self, face to face with Nature.

Thus the first condition for the tracing of a tableau
of Spanish contemporary literature appears to be
missing. There would be no composition in the picture,

no general lines, no connexion between the figures. Here a pensive, narcissus-like mind turns his back to Spanish tradition, and looks to the north for light in which to chisel his carefully thought-out phrases ; there a picturesque hidalgo, with the soul of a soldier and the face of a monk, seeks inspiration in the recesses of the national spirit, and style in the fastidious crafts-men of contemporary Italy and France ; a sensitive delicate artist delights in miniature renderings of Spanish things and people ; a powerful but somewhat rough man of letters seeks profit and honour in the supply of novels fitted for the general taste, according to the recognized tenets of French literary cooking ; a Basque rationalist lets fall novels of instinct and action with the self-ignorant spontaneity of the tree that lets fall its fruit ; while the most eminent of his country-men, in truly Wordsworthian isolation, keeps proving to himself and to his readers, by means of hard intel-lectual work, that the intellect does not matter, that instinct and vital force are the impulses which move the world, and that thought is but disguised desire ; open to all influences, from that of Ibsen to that of Franz Lehar ; the theatre lives in perfect anarchy, yet manages to preserve its strong national character ; and in poetry, the ever-living inspiration of the *Romancero* flourishes side by side with transplanta-tions from Verlaine, Walt Whitman, and Rabindranath Tagore.

Yet this very incoherence is in itself a typical feature of Spanish contemporary letters, and an analysis of it may lead to the discovery of still more pronounced characteristics. There is little doubt that the first cause which explains this dispersion of literary efforts is the strong individualistic bent of the Spanish people. The world of letters does not essentially differ in this respect from the world of politics, the world of commerce, or that of private relations. ' Each his own leader ' is a favourite norm of action in Spain. In this sense, therefore, the incoherence of Spanish literary life may be considered as permanent, since it is rooted in the national character. It is, however, modified by features of a transitory nature, which can only be rightly understood when taken in relation to the literary and educational evolution of the country.

Every nation evolves according to its own rhythm, determined in its turn by the interplay of national character and external conditions. But, leaving aside the vicissitudes of general history, the literary development of most nations reflects in its broken course the inner struggle between conflicting tendencies within the national character. Thus, in the history of English poetry are interwoven two conflicting tendencies, both distinctly typical of the English character, i. e. the æsthetical-pagan tendency, which can be found almost pure in Shakespeare, and the ethical-puritan tendency, strong in Milton and Shelley, predominant in Wordsworth. Thus, again, French literature owes much of its brilliancy and attractiveness to the interplay between the two shades of French intellectualism : the constructive classicism of Bossuet, Racine, and Montesquieu, and the dissolving, analytical spirit of Montaigne, Voltaire, and Anatole France ; two seemingly opposite varieties of one single spirit which are effectively combined in Pascal's *Lettres Provinciales*, or, again, in some of the comedies of Molière.

A similar fact occurs in Spanish literary history. But while in France and England the rhythm of literary development is determined by the conflict of two strong tendencies, in Spain it results from the lack of balance between the creative and the critical faculty of the race. The Spanish people are a pre-eminently passionate race, and their literature, therefore, evinces all the strength and all the weakness of passion. They are rich in those gifts which spring spontaneously from the subconscious depths of Nature; strong but irregular impulses; penetrating but unreliable instincts. They possess vision, divination, intuition, grace, and mother wit, power, grasp of reality, and a capacity for sudden discharges of almost unbounded energy. They are not, however, so well gifted in those qualities which are either the inherited capital or the hoarded-up treasure of the conscious self, such as speculative vigour, sustained and controlled feeling, and perseverance. A further illustration of the deep differences which distinguish the so-called ' Latin ' peoples. While France and Italy are eminently intellectual and critical, Spain is eminently intuitive and creative. And this predominance of the creative over the critical faculty is precisely the characteristic feature of Spanish literature and civilization.

Throughout Spanish literary history what is strong is the fruit of genius, what is weak is the work of talent. This is noticeable even in such fields of mental activity as philosophy and science, in which the contribution of Spain to the common fund of knowledge consists in brilliant and bold anticipation rather than in patient development. We would mention Vives, the precursor of Bacon; Servet, the precursor of Harvey; Vázquez Menchaca, the precursor of Grotius. But it becomes clearer in literature and the arts, where it explains the contrast between the vigour of spontaneous creation, guided by inspiration and instinct, and the feebleness of ' artistic ' attempts, regulated by doctrine and taste. No better illustration could be found for this contrast than Cervantes himself, who left us in *Don Quixote* models of his best and of his worst style—his best in those passages which he wrote when simply telling his tale and

letting his characters speak for themselves, his worst
when he stepped in himself, with his 'literary'
prejudices, and set out to give the world samples of
anthology Spanish. But it is not necessary to read
Spanish in order to observe this curious phenomenon
of Spanish psychology. There is in the National
Gallery as good an instance of it as *Don Quixote* itself
or the works of Calderón. I refer to the famous
'Venus and the Mirror' of Velázquez. It is a nude,
painted as only Velázquez could paint. So much for
the genius. But Velázquez had also to show the Court
of Philip IV that he had as good a talent as anybody for
representing an allegorical subject, and, therefore, his
delightful woman reclining on a couch was transformed into a Venus by the addition of a naked boy,
heavy, fat, and full of bread, provided with a pair of
wings, obviously insufficient to lift up to Olympus
such a solid, material little figure. The whole poised
in the most conventional, artificial style that could be
found in the studios and academies of Seville. Thus
the trappings of misguided talent often overdress the
effective simplicity of the Spanish genius.

Artists are seldom the best critics of their art. But
nowhere is this principle more general than in Spain.
The divorce between criticism and creation is with
us almost complete. It affects equally the critic,
to whom a certain dose of creative spirit is indispensable, and the creator, to whom the critical faculty
is a necessary instrument for expression. Thus the
Marqués de Santillana, an admirer of Petrarch, Dante,
and Boccaccio, despised that poetry, popular in its
inspiration and form, in which he left us the best of
his genius; Lope de Vega did not think so much of
his theatre as of his imitations of Ariosto; and
Cervantes, who prided himself no less on being the
author of *Persiles y Sigismunda* and of *Galatea* than
the creator of *Don Quixote*, never saw the true great-

ness of the masterpiece which his race had created through him. We may generalize and say that the writers of the Spanish Golden Century valued themselves for reasons quite other than those which inspire our own admiration for that wonderful period. They saw themselves as self-conscious artists, and judged their works according to somewhat academic rules of art after classical and Italian models. We consider the academic side of the Golden Century literature as a kind of by-product of the age, interesting, certainly, but by no means essential, nor even necessary, to its glory; while we admire in it that splendid wealth of creative impulse to which we owe the theatre, *Don Quixote*, the picaresque novels, and the literature of the mystics. So that, though the period was, in its own eyes, one of reading and scholarship, it has for us all the freshness of a self-ignorant primitive age.

It is a situation which, in varying degrees, occurs in all other periods of Spanish literary history, for in all of them the same divorce between the critical and the creative faculty is apparent. And this lack of balance between the genius and the intellect of the nation explains both the importance of the popular element in Spanish literature and the facility with which, in the course of history, Spain was overrun by waves of foreign influence.

The people are in all nations the most genuine representatives of the spontaneous tendencies of the race. When, therefore, as in Spain, these tendencies are predominant and constitute the main feature of the national character, the people are bound to play an important rôle in the development of the literature and art of the nation. That is what can be observed in the case of Spain. Time after time the taste of the cultivated class is led astray by foreign influences and fashions, or by scholarly prejudices. But the people's

instinct remains admirably faithful both to the
literary tradition of the country, and, what is far more
important, to artistic truth.   It is mainly due to the
consistency of the literary instinct of the people that
a continuous thread runs through the whole history of
Spanish literature, from the first epics to the romantic
school of the nineteenth century and certain varieties
of the poetry and theatre of the present day.   For
when the old epics were displaced in the favour of the
great by the learned poems (mester de clerecía), it
was the people's appetite for real epic poetry which
caused the growth of the old *Romancero*, as it were on
the ruins of the epic poems.   When the first Spanish
Italianates, disciples of Dante and Boccaccio, were
carried off their feet by the new Italian forms, it was
again the people's loyalty to the old romances—not
merely as forms, but because they were vessels too
straight and simple for the refined complications of
Italian poetry, and could hold nothing but the direct,
dramatic spirit of the race—which brought forth the
second crop of romances, thus providing a direct link
between the epic period and the dramatic period which
was about to set in during the sixteenth century.[1]
The Spanish drama, in its turn, was to a great extent
a popular creation.   The cultivated taste of the age
led towards a neo-classical theatre, in imitation of the
Greeks and in strict obedience to Aristotelian rules.
Popular favour, however, went to the plays which
disregarded the rules and revelled in romantic liberty.
Soon this tendency found its champion in Juan de la
Cueva and its poet in Lope de Vega.   But it is worth
while pointing out that Lope de Vega himself, who,
in his creative capacity, was the very incarnation of the
romantic spirit of the people, was by no means, as

[1] On this and other points of fact mentioned in this article see
L'Épopée castillane à travers la littérature espagnole, by Ramón
Menéndez Pidal.

a critic, so sure of his creed as might be expected. Far from it. In a somewhat depreciatory passage, which has become famous, he lays on the people ' who pay ' the responsibility for his own violations of the rules. Thus Lope the critic misunderstands Lope the creator, and indirectly shows how much the latter owed to the inspiring influence of the people. Sustained by the enthusiasm of the people for their favourite sport, the theatre lived as a creative force for nearly a century. Nor did its popularity abate when its development came to an end. When Calderón, the last of the great dramatists, disappeared, and the vicissitudes of political history working in secret harmony with the evolution of European thought placed Spanish culture under the direct influence of France, the Spanish people gave a fresh proof of the toughness of their national character. Critic after critic condemned the theatre of Lope, Tirso, and Calderón in the name of the principles which Boileau had defined with geometric precision in his *Art poétique*. Lope, Tirso, and Calderón, however, continued to be popular, much to the indignation of the learned gentlemen who preferred to them Voltaire and even Crébillon, so long as the three unities were respected. Towards the end of the eighteenth century the divergence between the instinct of the nation, true to itself, and its intellect, infatuated with foreign fashions, reached its maximum and gave rise to a truly paradoxical situation. The classicists succeeded in influencing the Government in their favour, and a law was passed prohibiting the representation of six hundred Spanish *comedias*, while the staging of new tragedies on the French model was subsidized by the State. But even this act of literary tyranny, so characteristic of the intellectual type of mind, was defeated by the passive resistance of the people. While the neo-classic tragedies were played before empty houses, the people flocked to hear the *sainetes* of Ramón de la Cruz, a new type of theatre which was in direct line with the Golden Century and which, though transformed, survives to this day, in the *género chico*.

Thus from the birth of our epics down to the present day the creative faculty of the nation evolves in a steady direction, according to the law of the national genius. It ignores or resists all intellectual dictation, and follows the instinct which prompts it to contemplate reality as it is and to interpret it freely and directly. This is the fact which gives to Spanish literature its independence, its originality, and its strong character.

The contrast is great between the steady development of Spain's creative impulse and the hesitating course of her culture. The national impulse which opposes to outside influences a vitality of its own, vigorous in her creative faculty, is weak or altogether absent in her intellectual life. From the philosophical point of view Spanish culture has its roots in latinity. But from the purely literary point of view Spanish culture, that is the conscious attitude of the learned towards works of art, starts under the influence of France. Vague and rudimentary as it no doubt was, the *art poétique* which prevailed when *Myo Cid* was written was, on the whole, French. Later on Italy dethroned France. Dante was to Santillana as exalted a figure as Virgil was to Dante; and Boccaccio came to be considered as a scholar of almost Aristotelian eminence. Favoured by historical circumstances, the Italian influence prevails all through the fifteenth and sixteenth centuries, reinforced, if anything, by the progress of classic studies. The great creators of the Golden Century, Cervantes, Lope, Góngora, Quevedo, consider themselves as humble disciples of the classic and of the Italian masters. The eighteenth century in Spain, as everywhere, belongs to France, and it is significant that in its last year the usual divorce between the intellect and the instinct of the country should have attained its maximum and culminated in the act of open hostility mentioned above. It would be foolish to deny that these successive influences under which Spanish culture found itself placed in the course of time, have played an important part in the literary development of the country. They have improved both the substance and the form of Spanish literature. They have countered the Spanish tendency toward self-absorption and isolation, and that attitude of inhibition before ideas for the sake of mere life and movement which is typical of Spanish art, with the opposite tendencies towards universality and ideological development which distinguish the Franco-Italian genius. They have also helped to correct the impatience and carelessness of the Spanish artist by setting before him models of form and high standards of literary finish. But the too-ready acceptance of foreign ideals of form has undoubtedly hindered the fusion of the conscious and scholarly with the unconscious and popular flow of art in Spanish literature.

The opinion may perhaps be risked that the distinctive feature of Spanish contemporary literature, and that which gives it a certain minimum of harmony and unity, is a more or less conscious effort towards achieving this fusion between the creative instinct and the cultivated intellect of the nation.

We must resist a strong temptation to place the origin of this effort at the Romantic period. It is true that Romanticism brought about a revival of interest in all Spanish subjects, the rejection of the three-unities standard and the return to the traditional liberty of our theatre. But these are only external and, some, accidental, features of Spanish art. What really typifies the creative spirit of Spain is its capacity

for turning into poetry immediate reality : for
painting on the very cloth of life as it is woven under
our eyes by the invisible hands of Time and Space.
The Spanish Romanticists were, in fact, but a new
generation of intellectuals, who, following the practice
of those elders whose theory they loudly rejected, had
fallen under a foreign artistic influence. This time
the influence was English [1]—Southey, Walter Scott,
Hookham Frere—and this time, instead of pointing
to Aristotle or Despréaux, it guided young Spaniards
towards *Myo Cid*, the *Romancero*, and the Golden
Century Theatre. The result was an art which sought
inspiration in Spanish historical legends, but not in
nature. It is only national externally, as consciously
traditional things generally are.

Yet there is something more than a mere confusion
between subject and substance in that feeling which
points to the Romantic period as the beginning of the
modern era in Spanish literature. First, Rivas with
his dramas, and, above all, Zorrilla with his legendary
poems, turned the attention of the literary public
towards the long-neglected Spanish past. The critics
began to be interested in Lope and Calderón. The
Romancero, which had never ceased to be *sung* by the
people (it still is) began to be *read* again. There might
be something in it, after all, since Monsieur Victor
Hugo admired it. And in this way began a familiarity
with the old models which had sooner or later to result
in a truer understanding of their spirit—that is, of
the creative spirit of Spain. Then the Romanticists
did useful work as iconoclasts. They cleared the
ground of many literary and æsthetical prejudices
and left it free for the activities of unfettered individual
genius. They were the first to benefit by their own

[1] The historical circumstance was the exile of a group of young
Spanish Liberals and their residence in London. Amongst them was
the leader of Spanish Romanticism, El Duque de Rivas.

work, and, within the Romantic movement, there may be observed a distinct progress from the imitation to the re-creation of Spanish art: thus in Zorrilla, from *El Puñal del Godo*, externally Spanish, to *Don Juan Tenorio*, in spirit and substance a true heir of *La Vida es Sueño* and *El Alcalde de Zalamea*.

But, considered as a whole, the Romantic movement does not essentially differ from previous periods of Spanish literature in its attitude towards the creative spirit of the race, and, as an intellectual or critical school, it is much more in harmony with foreign contemporary movements, such as French and English Romanticism, than with the true Spanish tradition which comes down, through the *Romancero* and the Theatre, from *Myo Cid*.

The movement towards incorporating the creative instinct of the race into the national culture—that is, towards the foundation of a Spanish culture truly deserving that name—is of more recent growth. In a sense it is but the natural result of the humanistic tendency of our age. Classical and Romantic, historic and futuristic ideas, are all for us but manifestations of the spirit of man, and in criticism no less than in economics we have at last come to believe that *there is no wealth but in life*. It may be, therefore, that even in this its last and saving movement the Spanish intellect is but following a lead come from abroad. At any rate, this time the lead is in the right direction, since modern criticism does but confirm old Spanish instinct in its adoption of life as the true criterion of art.

The present movement, not wholly conscious nor uniform nor deliberate, was heralded by a pioneering epoch in which three men stand out as the founders of contemporary Spanish culture : Giner, Menéndez y Pelayo, and Galdós.

Giner and Galdós are the subject of special articles in this volume. Don Marcelino Menéndez y Pelayo is the master of modern Spanish scholarship. In his relatively short life he managed to achieve an imposing task of critical research. He drew the tableau of Spanish literary life with a masterly hand, no less sure in the placing of the main lines and the judging of relative values than in the handling of the minutest details. He set up before Spain the reality of her literary past, with all the authority of his immense erudition and of his fine sense of criticism. He taught by example how to look objectively at national facts. And, fortunately, he left an excellent school of disciples.

There was no set co-operation between these three men, and I am, so far as I know, the first to connect their names in a constructive explanation of Spanish contemporary culture. Yet Giner, Menéndez y Pelayo, and Galdós undoubtedly are the symbols and standards respectively of the ethical, the critical, and the creative aspects of this culture. Symbols, because they incarnate the diffused spirit of the age, which obscurely groped towards a reassertion of Spanish values in their true relation to Europe and the world. Standards, because in them Spanish life, scholarship, and literature possess models which, being purely Spanish, are yet universal and modern, that is human and free.[1]

We are now in a position to attempt a summary of the chief characteristics of Spanish contemporary literature. For the first time, thanks to the favourable spirit of the age, humanistic and free from prejudice, the intellect of the country seems to beat in sympathy with the creative instinct traditional in the race. Not

[1] This would perhaps apply in a lesser degree to Menéndez y Pelayo, whose mind was somewhat hindered in its movements by a closely guarded Catholic orthodoxy. Yet there is no doubt that he always strove to, and often succeeded in, overcoming this limitation when engaged in critical work.

that traces of the intellectualist tendency are wholly absent. The same type of mind which in the eighteenth century condemned Calderón in the name of Boileau, and in the sixteenth condemned Lope in the name of Aristotle, inspires nowadays rigidly imitated *pastiches* of Cervantes. Similarly, the same *literary* ambition which led even great men like Cervantes to imitate Sannazaro inspires in lesser men than Cervantes imitations of Oscar Wilde. There is, moreover, in the Spanish intellect an innate tendency towards breaking loose from reality—perhaps a reaction against the realism of the Spanish instinct. It is the weak side of the Spanish variety of fancy which goes by the name of *ingenio*. The present movement runs, therefore, counter to both innate and acquired intellectual ways, and cannot be expected to make much progress without provoking eddies and countercurrents. But the main current undoubtedly leads towards a straightforward interpretation of reality which is in line with the true creative spirit of the Spanish classics.

I have spoken of a main current. An undercurrent would have been a better image, for, though the present tendency towards spiritual realism is general—at any rate, among the best—the ways in which this aim is sought and attained are as numerous as the individual writers afield. We are again at our point of departure, confronted with that incoherence and dispersion of effort typical of Spanish literature and art, and which we found then to be rooted in the individualism of the race. But we can now give yet another cause of it. We know that the mainspring in the literature of the country is a creative, genius-like spirit. It is the law of such a spirit that it seeks reality direct and not in its reflection on culture. Just as the critical spirit feeds on books, the creative spirit feeds on living facts and feelings. It follows that the Spanish writer, even though he reads the works of his contemporaries, is not passive enough to let his neighbours influence him. That is why the literary atmosphere is rarefied, and the individualistic tendency finds little check in social modes of thought.

A certain underlying unity results, however, from a common tendency towards seeking inspiration in human nature as seen through Spanish contemporary reality. The people continue to be a prominent factor in the literary life of the nation. They remain the race of spontaneous poets to whom we owe the old epic *Romancero* and that other lyrical ' *Romancero* ', no less admirable if less known, the priceless treasure of Spanish popular songs.[1] Moreover, the wealth of poetical ore which they possess makes them excellent subjects for literary treatment, and thus they contribute, passively with their lives no less than actively with their songs, to that transformation of present-day reality into poetry which is, and always was, the distinctive characteristic of Spanish literature. The most typical example of this double influence of the people on present-day art is to be found in the Theatre, and particularly in that peculiar variety of it called *género chico*. The very name (small *genre*) is an apposite instance of the intellectualist attitude towards genuine Spanish creations. Your intellectual playwright prefers to imitate Ibsen or Bernard Shaw, but the audiences, ' who pay ', prefer the *género chico*, and so the author sighs and writes little marvels for the stage. The *género chico* is no doubt a chaotic type of theatre, vague and free enough to admit the classical masterpiece, the sentimental Viennese ineptitude, and the Parisian *déshabillé* sketch. In this, as in its self-ignorance and in its admirable vitality, it resembles the Golden Century *comedia*.

[1] See my essay on Spanish Popular Poetry in *Shelley and Calderón and other Essays*, Constable, 1920.

A similar orientation towards a spiritual realism in harmony with the deepest instinct of the race can be observed in all the other literary *genres*. It inspires the poetry of the brothers Machado as well as the novels of Baroja, the poems and novels of Pérez de Ayala as well as the admirable sketches of Azorín, the essays of Ortega as well as the innumerable newspaper articles into which Maeztu has poured his mind born for more permanent tasks ; it is the very essence of the art of Valle Inclán, poet, novelist, and playwright, and the comfort and discomfort of that unequal, solitary, and self-torturing genius, Unamuno. Thus Spanish contemporary literature may achieve the fusion of the intellect and the instinct of the race, and lead to a culture which would add to its vital creative vigour, intellectual consistency, self-confidence, and a capacity for harmonious development.

BENITO PÉREZ GALDÓS

I⊤ is generally assumed that men of genius are rarely recognized during their lifetime. Whatever its merits so far as other countries are concerned, this pessimistic view can hardly be said to apply to Spain. It would be difficult to find a great name in the history of Spanish letters which had to wait for death in order to conquer immortality. Cervantes saw *Don Quixote* a famous book years before he took the trouble to write its second and better half. Lope de Vega was for the greater part of his life the idol of Madrid. In our own days, Galdós has tasted the wine of glory— he delighted in it with his usual, almost childish relish for pleasure—and has seen himself acclaimed by his contemporaries as the greatest literary genius which Spain has produced since the Golden Century.

The reason for this instant recognition of genius by the Spanish public is not far to seek. It is twofold. On the one hand, the Spanish genius, even when universal in its essence, is strongly national in its manner and attire. On the other hand, it is creative, that is, it derives its strength from deep sources of inspiration and instinct, and therefore appeals directly to the very centre of understanding without having to reach our being through the devious road of the intellect. Hence, what it says is never caviare to the general, but the very substance of the general soul which recognizes itself in the work of genius and appreciates it instantly. That is why Galdós achieved popularity during his lifetime. He is, like our great classics, a creator.

Spain invented the novel, and one of the three original types of theatre which the western world knows. Galdós is, therefore, in the true line of Spanish literary tradition, since he is above all a novelist with a strong dramatic tendency. The whole of his work can indeed be placed in a zone intermediate between the novel and the drama, for his novels are markedly dramatic and his dramas evolve with the vital continuity of novels.

The novel may be defined as the æsthetic expression of life, and this definition naturally leads to a division of the study of a novelist into three heads, namely, the scope of his work, the quality of his æsthetic attitude, and his style ; or, in other words, the subject, the artist, and the medium. It is hardly necessary to add that such a division cannot be understood nor even imagined literally. Matter, manner, and attitude in the work of an artist are as inseparable as body, soul, and environment in the life of a man. But it is the law of our intellect that, in order to analyse it must unfold in succession things that strike the mind at one and the same time, and so, at the risk of repetition, I shall deal in turn with each of these three aspects of Galdós's artistic personality.

The subject of Galdós's work could be defined thus ; human nature as seen by an unprejudiced observer of nineteenth-century Spain.

Galdós's knowledge of Spain is complete and all-embracing. From this point of view—as from many others—he is the only truly national writer of the nineteenth century. Pereda belongs to a region, the Montaña ; Valera belongs to a class, the refined aristocracy ; Blasco Ibáñez is in manner and mind a cosmopolitan, if not a French, novelist. Galdós is Spanish, and he covers the whole of Spain, every province of its territory, every layer of its population, every shadow of its thought, and we may add, every year of its nineteenth century.

Curiously enough, this literary knight-errant of Spain was born in a land which only by a constitutional fiction can be considered as a part of the Peninsula. He saw the light in the Canary Islands, in 1845. But birth is an accident. From the age of twenty Galdós belongs to Madrid, and it is Madrid which he describes most willingly, and with a love which years of intimate knowledge did not abate. From his first work, *La Fontana de Oro* (1870) we begin to see under our eyes the unwieldy irregular town, full of an excitable and good-humoured population ; its vast aristocratic mansions, low masses of granite and brick ; its blocks of flats in which every *patio* is like a small village, bubbling with gossip and quarrels ; its irregular, ill-paved streets which, like rivers dying in sands, radiate towards the desert over which, as our author says, ' the heavens rise as spiritual life over the aridity of asceticism '.[1] But, though prominent in his books, Madrid takes no more important a place in them than it does in the life of the nation, and Galdós has succeeded in rendering with equal vividness and felicity the atmosphere of other Spanish towns, whether he conceals their features under an assumed name, as with his ' Ficóbriga' in *Gloria* or his ' Orbajosa ' in *Doña Perfecta*, or reveals their whole identity down to the most vivid details of everyday life, as in his admirable rendering of Toledo in *Angel Guerra*. His knowledge of town and country is precise and detailed. Thus, he compares ' the sudden harsh, strident outbursts of laughter ' of one of his characters in *Lo Prohibido* to ' the tearing of cloth which one hears when passing along the Calle de Postas in shopping hours ', a line which makes one pause and dream of his tall, gaunt figure, stealing along the streets of Madrid, a smile on his thin lips, his eyes lost in that waking

---

[1] *La Familia de León Roch*, i.

dream of born observers, in which the mind is at rest but the instinct is alert and watching.

As he watched the life of the town and heard the tearing of cloth in the Calle de Postas, so he seems to have witnessed the life of the whole country during that nineteenth century which will perhaps some day be considered as the true Renaissance of Spain. Spain, like England, placed in the suburbs of Europe, has had a life of her own, subject to a historical rhythm quite different from that of the rest of the continent. Thus though the pioneer of municipal and parliamentary institutions in Europe, Spain arrives at the gates of the nineteenth century in a belated phase of development. Now the nineteenth century is in the history of Spain the constitutional century, not merely in the political, but in the national and cultural sense of the word. It is in the nineteenth century, through a calvary of civil wars, that Spain attains at last a full consciousness of her being. During the nineteenth century, Spain had to assimilate not only the French Revolution, but the Renaissance, and such elements of the Reformation as were not repugnant to her genius. It is a chaotic period of wars, which devastated the body no doubt but certainly stimulated the spirit of the nation. Galdós began to write almost exactly when the Bourbon Restoration initiated a period of relative stability, in reality the last phase of the struggle. He could look back on a vast field of romantic material which only awaited a great artist to be fashioned into immortal works. He saw his opportunity and proved himself worthy of it.

His *Episodios Nacionales* are indeed an imposing work. All this romantic material of the nineteenth century is turned to account, from Trafalgar (the title of the first episode) to the beginnings of the present reign. In these forty-six volumes, many of which are admirable, and none of which can be passed over,

Galdós gave us the history of Spain as seen from the drawing-room of contemporaries, not from the study of the historian. It is a living history, not the historical novel in the somewhat grandfatherly manner of Erckmann-Chatrian, nor again in the romantic and even romanesque manner of Walter Scott, but a vivid and dramatic interpretation of the life of the people through the events of the century, their hopes, feelings, thoughts, and disappointments.

Apart from their literary merit, the *Episodios Nacionales* have been one of the most important elements in the formation of a Spanish national consciousness. Galdós was and is the most widely read of Spanish writers. His influence as an educator of the Spanish mind is incalculable.

A similar value must be attached to his non-historical novels,[1] a series of thirty works the subject of which is the life of the Spanish people during the last quarter of the nineteenth century.

But though his immediate and concrete subject is the Spaniard of his age, his essential object is man. His outlook is human. If his characters are Spanish it is because creation is concrete and the Spanish genius never creates *ex nihilo* but from nature. His Spaniards, however, are as universal as those of Cervantes, for their life is woven with the eternal threads of love, destiny, and death.

If the novel is an aesthetic interpretation of life, it follows that novels may fail as works of art if conceived under ethical or intellectual preconceptions. Cervantes, it is generally admitted, set to work with an express ethical purpose when he wrote his *Don Quixote*. Fortunately, however, his creative instinct burst through his ethical intentions, and, as he pro-

[1] His first novel, *La Fontana de Oro* is a kind of *Episodio Nacional* and can hardly be called non-historical.

ceeded, his end—the satire on chivalry books—soon
became the means, while the means, the type of *Don
Quixote*, became the real subject of the book and
made it immortal.

Intellectual preconceptions were not yet strong in
Cervantes' age. They had to wait till the nineteenth
century, when Émile Zola tried to transform the novel
into a branch of Natural History, closely connected
with veterinary science.

Galdós is almost a pure novelist, that is, he is almost
free from both ethical and intellectual preconceptions.
Yet, not quite. There is in him a strong political
passion which now and then breaks out and upsets his
artistic impartiality. His famous anti-clerical series—
Doña Perfecta, Gloria, La Familia de León Roch—
though admirable novels, are undoubtedly written
in a spirit of passion and partisanship. This spirit was
strong in him, since it inspired his famous play *Electra*
in 1901, twenty-three years after the publication of
León Roch. Yet the evolution from *Doña Perfecta* to
León Roch shows a gradual refinement of his ethical
preconception and an effort to raise the conflict of
religious prejudices to the level of tragedy.

As for intellectual preconceptions, Galdós victori-
ously resisted the influence of his great French contemporary and never tried to turn his art into
a science, probably because, fortunately, the notion
that such a transformation could be an improvement
of art could not enter his Spanish head. The pathetic
belief in science which for several decades shed
a melancholy light over the age, left however its mark
on Galdós's work. We can see it in the choice of his
heroes, who often, particularly in his first manner,
belong to the noble scientist type—his José Rey, his
León Roch, both mathematicians, astronomers, geolo-
gists. But Galdós is always greater than his creations,
and it would be a mistake to imagine that his outlook

was limited to that of his scientific characters, however noble and open-minded he portrayed them. He was saved from the religion of science by his sense of humour.

At bottom, and when he is writing free from the direct influence of public events, his work is purely aesthetic. Many of his friends have reproached him for his artistic impartiality, which they call impassivity. He knew best. He was true to his vocation, and true to the literary tradition of Spain, which from its earliest epics to its picaresque novel and to *Don Quixote*, has contemplated life with an artistic serenity rivalled only by the calm attitude of Shakespeare, the pole-star and model of all true artists. It is because he was able to look upon life with eyes clean from prejudice and kindled with love that his creations are so true. He has that universal sympathy of poetic souls—souls, that is, which carry within them the whole world.

A writer possessing that virtue can impart a permanent and universal value to any subject upon which he may chance to touch. Glimpses of Galdós's inner poetical vision shine here and there in his style, shedding a ray of light on the humblest, apparently most unimportant, facts; little touches which do not in the least disturb the quiet pace of the narrative, yet give it nobility and deepen and widen the interest of the plot, in which, we feel, God and nature and destiny are present and co-operate.

From such depth of intuition his characters are created. We must not go to him for that skilful analysis, that chemistry of the human soul, into which the modern novel seems to degenerate under the influence of intellectual culture and progress. Galdós's characters are not dissected, but alive, and they give us their actions, not their motives.

It follows that his art is mainly dramatic. Galdós

has given Spain and the world a splendid galaxy of
characters, creatures of flesh and blood who are known
to us body and soul and quickly become familiar figures
in our national life. In the skill and vigour of his
dramatic developments he can stand comparison with
any novelist old or new. He excels in the knitting
of events into crises of admirable emotional strength,
by means which are within the bounds of good taste
and never fall into melodrama. Let us mention for
instance the murder of Ángel Guerra, a *dénouement* as
inevitable, and yet as skilfully brought to its close
almost by surprise as the death of Othello. Galdós's
dramatic ability, though not without a certain astute-
ness, is, however, essentially different from that almost
mechanical ingeniousness with which Calderón con-
trived his plays. A novel of Galdós is to a play of
Calderón what an organism is to a mechanism. In
Galdós the crisis is brought about by the interplay
of external circumstances and character. This non-
interference before events leads him sometimes to
awkward, almost childish inability of exposition, which
is particularly observable in his plays.

Galdós's characters are not static. They grow,
evolve, and develop as the work proceeds. And
this tendency towards emphasizing growth probably
explains why, though born above all a dramatist, he
should have devoted most of his time to novel-writing.
He undoubtedly found the modern stage—as Shakespeare himself would have done—too narrow for the
delineation of character along the line of time. Our
theatre has gradually contracted along the dimension
of time. The last phase of this evolution is the
Cinema, in spirit, no less than in matter, a mere film.
The characters in Galdós are not cinematographic.
They live and develop, and in this he is superior to all
Spanish classics except Cervantes.

It goes without saying that since Galdós can make

his characters develop, he knows them from within, and penetrates into the depths of their instinct and impulses. He puts in the mouth of one of his most admirable types, Ángel Guerra, a significant word of his own coining : *impulsología*. No better name could be given to the branch of psychology that he knew best. There is little of the human underworld which he did not fathom and express with Wordsworthian penetration and felicity, and, in a sense, the whole of his work may be interpreted as the drama of impulse lurking under the comedy of action.

This central idea explains several of the most prominent features of his art, and particularly his frequent recourse to dreams and apparitions. With Galdós, dreams are not mere tricks for melodramatic effect. They are intimately linked up with the psychology of the character who dreams them, and act as small explosions from the subconscious, which throw up to the surface of consciousness shapeless fragments of the material below. In this, of course, Galdós anticipates the modern views of psycho-analysis. His treatment of dreams must be related to that of forebodings, or, as the Spanish language admirably says, *corazonadas*. The most famous instance of this is perhaps the secret expectancy with which Gloria, in the novel of this name, feels the arrival of Daniel, the unknown chosen of her heart who, without her knowing it, is being saved from the tempest by the priest of the parish while she is at prayer in the church. Another aspect of Galdós's ' impulsological ' manner is his tendency to picture those revulsions of character which take place when a natural group of tendencies has been repressed by education, environment, or self-deception and is suddenly released by a shock of fact giving back in one second all the energy locked up for years in the under-soul. Such dramatic reversions to type occur in practically every book of Galdós. In his very first novel, written when he was twenty-five, there is an admirable instance in Doña Paulita, the mystical bigot who has wasted her youth in what she thought to be divine love only to find her bigotry suddenly burnt away in the fire of her worldly love for Lázaro. The case of Ángel Guerra is similar in its essentials though treated with more subtlety. Ángel Guerra begins with worldly love, deviates towards mysticism under the fascination of his platonic mistress, the beautiful nun Leré, then, on his death-bed, murdered while in the exercise of a beautiful act of charity, he confesses that he has been the victim of self-delusion and that, all through, he loved Leré with earthly love. In the same novel, most skilfully arranged in parallel pattern with the case of Ángel Guerra, will be found the case of Don Tomé, the innocent, almost uncorporeal saint, who dies, also assisted by Leré, also in love with her, confessing his pure unearthly love to Ángel Guerra in terms of singular warmth expressive of ardent desire.

It is this wealth of impulse which gives his world its wonderful vigour. With him, weakness itself seems overflowing with vitality. In one of his best novels, *Fortunata y Jacinta*, Galdós has left us a type of a neurotic assistant chemist, of delicate body, average mind, and but little will, a type which it would seem almost impossible to endow with interest. Yet, he has made it live and move so admirably, with such abundance of motive and impulse, such variety of shades of feeling and passion, that Maxi is one of the great creations of the nineteenth century.

This creative miracle is due to the magic power of love. Galdós loved his characters, and that is why he saw into them. The people, quick to seize spiritual facts, had nicknamed him ' El Abuelo ' (the Grand-father). It was a true instinct which gave him that name. In the eyes of the Spanish people, Galdós stands surrounded by a crowd of living progeny—

saints, adventurers, sweet maids, intriguers, passionate mothers, wives, and mistresses, criminals, and the motley variety of less definite types, all creatures whom he loved as the children of his heart, and in whom he will live as long as the Spanish language is spoken.

Galdós would not be a Spanish creative genius if he had taken the trouble to write well. No great Spaniard ever did. The style of great Spanish works reflects the influence of two conflicting tendencies : that of the creative instinct of the race and that of the literary preconceptions of the age. The first, a natural tendency, leads the writer to disregard mere form and to concentrate on the living substance. The second, an acquired tendency, checks the free flow of expression, and in extreme cases, as in the later development of Góngora or Calderón, overburdens the style with ornament.

There are now and then in Galdós traces of this unfortunate influence of literary preconceptions over style. At times, he seems to be trying to imitate Cervantes, as for instance in the opening chapters of *Doña Perfecta.* Later he passed through a fever of inversions. But, despite these witnesses to a national failing which could not be wholly absent from a writer so typically Spanish, Galdós's style flows clear like a river from a spring of creative inspiration. He is too great to treat style as more than a mere medium of expression. The cultivation of diction for the sake of diction is a sign of decadence, that is, of impotence ; and we know that Galdós was anything but impotent. His prose is like a sail, more or less full according to the strength of the wind of inspiration. When he is moved, no one writes better ; when he is dealing with unimportant facts or fulfilling those menial tasks which are necessary in dramatic and narrative litera-

ture, he lets expression fall to the simple level of the
occasion. He is above all sincere and true.

With him, expression is subordinate to impression ;
words are tools. This is why we must not go to him
for landscapes. His interest is in man, and to nature
he gives exactly the same place which the painters of
the Spanish school gave it, namely, the background.
Not that his feeling for nature is poor or defective.
Few writers speak of natural life with more sympathy
and penetration than Galdós. But, being an eminently
dramatic genius, he could not suspend the development
of his action in order to indulge in a kind of pictorial
intermezzo. He has left few but splendid descriptions
of natural events, tempests, shipwrecks, sunsets. . . .
But in these cases nature finds a place in the action
as one of the characters thereof, and her intervention
is admirably timed to the enhancement of dramatic
interest. Moreover, the Galdosian bend towards
picturing concrete persons leads him to attribute to
trees, plains, rivers, and even buildings, human
motives and attitudes. An excellent example of all
these features of Galdós's treatment of nature will
be found in the description of the tempest in *Gloria*.
Nine-tenths of his style is the style of his characters,
and in this, as in his interpretation of impulse, our
great novelist shows how Protean his nature was.
Just as he describes his characters by their own actions,
so he expresses them by their own words. Often
indeed, even in his early novels, the narrative form is
dropped altogether and the characters are left to
speak in dialogue, the author putting in a rare occasional
indication as to gesture, voice, or attitude, mere stage
directions. There are novels—*El Abuelo* is a typical
example—which are written in this form from beginning to end, a kind of writing which has no less a precedent than *La Celestina*. At other times Galdós
develops part or the whole of the novel (*La Estafeta*

Romántica, for instance) in the form of letters pur-
ported to be written by the persons in the story,
another direct, dramatic way of letting the characters
speak for themselves. And it is not only what his
characters say, but the manner and form of their
speech, which is theirs and living. He has worked so
deep in this respect that, though he delighted in the
presentation of urban types, whose tendency to slang
is strong in all nations, his books have lost nothing of
their power and freshness with years. For Galdós
knew how to penetrate below the surface in language
no less than in action, and, without losing in liveliness,
to reach a level of expression which, being true, is in
the real sense of the word classic. Now and then, and
for purposes of illustration, he turns to account those
little oddities of speech with which it is easy to give
a type a certain external consistence, or a silhouette,
such as the verbal infelicities of Mrs. Malaprop. But,
in general, he seeks adequacy in language by the direct
expression of character. As his own style flows from
inspiration, his characters speak from the outpourings
of their heart. Hence his simplicity and strength.
Hence, also, his variety. His style is like a clear river
which flows always even and the same, yet reflects
whatever skies there are overhead in the author's mind.

In its dramatic quality, in its carelessness, in its
swiftness, and in its humble subordination to the substance of action, Galdós's style is therefore classically
Spanish. There is another Spanish quality which
can be found in it to an eminent degree, namely,
the power of forcible and condensed expression. A
passage in *Doña Perfecta* may be given as an example.
It is the last scene of the book. Midnight. While
Rosario, Doña Perfecta's daughter, the victim of her
mother's bigotry, is revealing to her in a moment of
weakness that she has arranged to run away that night
with José Rey, Remedios, the priest's sister, who wants

Rosario to marry her son and feels a strong hatred
against Rosario's lover, arrives at the house eager to
impart to Doña Perfecta that José is in the garden,
hidden, waiting for Rosario. She knocks at the front
door. This is the way Galdós puts it :

Rosario was on her knees. At that moment, they heard three
knocks, three explosions. It was the heart of Remedios knocking
at the door.

An admirable synthesis of the state of mind of
Remedios, the action of her hand and the beating of
her passionate heart in her breast. Such examples
abound in Galdós's novels and dramas. They contribute to give his work its classical flavour.

In Spanish literature Galdós ranks as the greatest
novelist since Cervantes. He has not created a type
as universal as Don Quixote, but then Don Quixote
is unique. He has, on the other hand, over Cervantes
the advantage of three centuries of European life, so
that he moves with greater philosophic and literary
liberty ; and, in these three centuries, perhaps the
greatest event in literature—Shakespeare.

In European literature Galdós undoubtedly deserves
to rank with the great novelists of the century, in line
with Dickens, Balzac, and Dostoievsky.

A comparison between Galdós and Dickens has
become quite customary in Spanish criticism. The
two names are naturally related in the mind of the
Spanish reader because Galdós is rich in humour, and
Dickens owes perhaps most of his foreign popularity
to his humorous vein. But, if I may venture a personal
opinion which may not find ready acceptance, the
comparison between Dickens and Galdós is not so much
an honour to Galdós as an honour to Dickens. Galdós
is superior to Dickens because his humour arises out
of human, universal conditions, while Dickens's

humour arises out of a social or conventional setting. Dickens deliberately mixes the comic element in the composition of his fables.   In Galdós, humorous situations naturally result from the interplay of circumstance and character.   Moreover, Galdós easily reaches that high pinnacle of dramatic art which Shakespeare and Cervantes alone were great enough to attain before him, namely, the interweaving of comic and tragic in one and the same scene and even in one and the same person.   Many of his characters in fact live in a zone of changing lights, comic and tragic, and move to tears and laughter at the same time—thus, Maxi in *Fortunata y Jacinta*, Don Pio in *El Abuelo*, and Pepet in *La Loca de la Casa*.   It is doubtful whether Dickens ever rose to such heights of dramatic conception.   Rather than tragic, his outlook might not unfairly be described as melodramatic.

With Balzac, the comparison suggests itself because Galdós wrote a real *Comédie Humaine* in a Spanish setting.   His inferiority to the French master lies perhaps in that his works are more easy-going, and have in them less of that intensity, that appetite for life which is the secret of Balzac's creative power. Balzac is the more vigorous of the two, Galdós perhaps the better artist and certainly the more lovable mind.

Galdós resembles Dostoievsky in his preference for that zone of human nature where subliminal forces work obscurely in the shaping of action and character. As with Dostoievsky, his characters are often highly strung and at times unhinged.   Maxi, Nazarin, are true Dostoievskian types.   Both the Spaniard and the Russian seem to have a foible for depicting mystics and madmen.   There is a Spanish saying that ' children and madmen tell the truth '.   It is in search of truth that Dostoievsky and Galdós go to their abnormal types of humanity, hoping thus to evade the strict censorship of reason.   Their main

interest is in destiny. They are not so much concerned
with man in his relation to society as with man in his
relation to Eternity, and they instinctively feel that
it is in exploring the subconscious depths that glimmers
of truth may be seen shining here and there in moments
of crisis. Hence their common preoccupation with
religion. The three anti-clerical novels of Galdós are
little more than a preliminary phase of his religious
obsession, during which he, as it were, clears the
ground of all political prepossessions before starting
on his really religious work. He seems to have a
marked preference for the mystical-practical type
which St. Teresa immortalized and of which he gave
such a lovable rendering in his Sor Lorenza or Leré in
Angel Guerra. But he has studied almost every possible
variety of the type with his usual penetration and
impartiality.

Galdós does not reach the poignancy of Dostoievsky's tortured questionings. There is nothing in his
work to compare with the tragedy of Ivan Karamazov.
But he is calmer and more serene. This is due first
to his Spanish common sense. In the Spaniard there
is always a Sancho along with a Don Quixote, as
Santa Teresa herself brilliantly proved by her own life.
Then, the Spanish genius shuns that almost morbid
tendency towards analysis which made Dostoievsky
unhappy and his novels bibles of desperation. What
in Dostoievsky is a problem, ever present to the intellect, never transcends in Galdós the aesthetic plane, and
remains a tacit sense of tragedy contemplated in silence
like the black heavens in a moonless night. Dostoievsky, moreover, never found an answer to his
questionings, and to the end remained haunted by
his unsolved problem of destiny. Galdós found in
his nature a living answer which satisfied him. Galdós
is the novelist of love.

The whole of his work is an illustration of the forms

that love may take in the world, its triumphs, failures, disguises and transformations, its wanton playfulness and deep but fleeting joys. He is far from giving a rose-coloured version of love and life. Many of his novels—perhaps most of them—end in utter disappointment, despair, death. As if he wanted to prove how far he is convinced that love is a wanton, senseless passion, he shows in *Fortunata y Jacinta* a triangle of unrequited love : on each side, a man in love with a woman and these two women both in love with a third man, while this third man, the apex on which all these lines of love converge, is a perfectly inane creature who seems incapable of loving anybody. Yet the book is not cynical, nor pitiless, nor pessimistic, nor tragic. It is full of human sympathy and so overflowing with vitality that one shuts it after the death of Jacinta and the locking up of Maxi in a lunatic asylum with the sense that life is worth living when people can die and go mad in such a way.

Galdós, however, has no theory about love and does not claim to hold the secret of any panacea. With him love is not an idea but a living feeling which pervades all his work. He brings to Spanish literature a quality which is not very abundant in it, a delicate tenderness, wholly free from sentimentality, particularly noticeable when he speaks of children. No other writer ever treats children with so delightful a touch, light, tender, a little humorous. He speaks in *Gloria* of the sexton's little boy with ' his dirty little fingers like rose leaves fallen in mud '. In *León Roch*, when relating the infancy of María Egipciaca and her brother, he describes how, in imitation of St. Teresa, they decided to run away in order to perish as martyrs at the hands of the Infidels, and adds : ' they fell asleep under the protection of a rock, and there, the Maker of all things, God Omnipotent, gave them a kiss and delivered them into the hands of the constabulary.'

He knew, therefore, what he was saying when in the mouths of so many of his characters he put words which expressed his faith in love as the one positive force of the world, the one force which made life worth living and unhappiness itself desirable. He looked on all forms of love with mystic eyes, and saw them as forms of the eternal love of God. ' The love of God—he says in *León Roch*—is nothing but the sublimation of the love of his creatures.' Ángel Guerra, on his death-bed, sums up this philosophy in words of admirable simplicity : ' The only thing one gets out of this life is the pleasure and the joy of loving.' And Pepa Fúcar, in *León Roch*, when asked to renounce her happiness for conscience' sake, has force enough while bowing to destiny to utter this eloquent protest : ' My conscience is to love.' An adaptation of this phrase might do for a brief description of Galdós's work : his art was love.

NOTE ON DON FRANCISCO
GINER DE LOS RÍOS

It is a typical feature of our age that in it the
remedies for the ills of the body politic are sought in
scientific re-arrangements—whether of an economic,
a juridical, or a mechanical order. No one seems to
realize that the ' body ' politic has in fact no other ills
than those of its soul, and that it is in the spirit that
the cure for all social evils must be found. It follows
that the great men of the age are politicians, scientists,
and engineers, while the sage, the master, and the
saint live and die ignored by the mass. I believe that
Spain can claim the distinction of possessing a truer
instinct in this respect than most other nations.
She was ever an admirer of her saints, even in times
when belief was tainted with superstition, and in our
day she has worshipped with a purer and clearer and
more human love the saint who inspired the contemporary revival of Spanish education—Don Francisco Giner.

Don Francisco, as he was universally known, was
born in 1839, in the little town of Ronda, famous for
its picturesque situation between Granada and Málaga.
He was, on his mother's side, related to the family of
Ríos Rosas, which had been made famous in Spanish
politics by his uncle, Don Antonio. Having studied
law in the universities of Barcelona and Granada, he
came to Madrid in 1863, and in three years' time he
acquired so much prestige among the best and most
advanced intellects of the period, that when, in 1866,
he won the Chair of Jurisprudence in the University
of Madrid, serious objections were raised in official

quarters where thought was then considered suspect. He was, however, appointed, and became one of the most convinced disciples of Sanz del Río, his predecessor in the leadership of Spanish educational thought and himself a disciple of Krause. In 1867 Sanz del Río resigned his chair, rather than submit to a declaration of religious, political, and even dynastical faith, which the notorious minister Orovio sought to impose upon him. Giner followed his master with a little band of die-hards, all of whom had to wait until 1868 to recover their posts, in which they were reinstated by the Revolutionary Government.

But in 1875 Orovio came back to power with the Restoration. The attack on the freedom of the chair was renewed. It was answered in a similar fashion by the disciples of Sanz del Río (who had died in 1869). Giner, deprived of his chair, was imprisoned in Cádiz, where he received the visit of the English Consul, come to offer him the help of British public opinion. Giner politely but firmly declined all foreign help. He soon recovered his liberty, though not his chair, but the incident proved a blessing in disguise. He naturally became the leader of the little group of dismissed professors, and of that group was born what was to become one of the most important instruments for the regeneration of Spanish education, i.e. the *Institución Libre de Enseñanza*. The Institución, by which short title it is known everywhere in Spain, is an educational establishment free from all interference of Church or State, and, in it, Giner was able to apply his doctrines on education, to act upon the people of Spain in a far more effective manner than through mere political speeches, and to provide a model school, not merely for Spain, but even, in many ways, for the whole of Europe. Moreover, the Institución helped Giner to find out his own true vocation. From that moment he became a teacher of teachers.

The main influences which acted on his conception of education were German and English. As is but natural, the German influence was theoretical and philosophical, while the English was personal and positive. The first may be summed up in one name : Krause. The philosophy of Krause inherently appeals to Spaniards more perhaps than to other races. This may be due to the positive element in it, the tendency never to lose sight of the fact that the real aim of all philosophy is life itself. Its expansion in Spain was further favoured by the ability and enthusiasm of Professor Sanz del Río. It was from Sanz del Río that Giner took his ideas and, as it were, the foundations of his educational philosophy. For Don Francisco had no tradition to go upon when starting on his adventure, and it was necessary for him to begin at the beginning. That is perhaps why he succeeded so well ; for, being unhindered by precedents, he simply took for his guide the principle that all education must be human, and not merely national or civic. In this he was helped by his English proclivities. He had excellent friendships in England, and soon learnt to appreciate the intellectual and moral refinement of a certain type of English home. He was quick to understand the education value of sports and collegiate life, as he saw it in Eton, and during his stay at Balliol with Jowett. But it is a mark of his greatness that, whilst assimilating all the tendencies of fellowship and character formation which give its permanent value to English education, he remained wholly free from the class prejudice and the snobbishness, both intellectual and social, with which, rightly or wrongly, English education is sometimes associated.

The need for a far-reaching reform in Spanish educational methods was then urgent. The Spanish universities, which up to the sixteenth century had stood in the first rank of European culture, had since then fallen so low that they hardly counted as educational forces in the country, and, but for the value of individual efforts here and there, might have been closed altogether without any loss to the nation. Spain had lost her Catholic culture, but had evolved nothing in its place. All was to be built anew. Don Francisco realized the position in all its gravity, but he did not, like others, yield to pessimism and despair, perhaps because, unlike others, he took a long view and knew how to be patient. He never swerved from the conviction that the main task was not to be found in administration, organization, or endowment, but in men. And it was to the making of men that he devoted his life.

It is indeed as a maker of men that he will keep his high position in the history of his country. Nor could he have succeeded in his task had he been a mere pedagogue. Pedagogy was with him simply an outlet for the rich stream of life which poured into his soul through action and contemplation. He had a keen love of nature. Before the days of the ' open air ' cult, he was an indefatigable walker, a hardy mountaineer, fearless of the snows and treacherous winds of Guadarrama, never happier than when chance made him stay the night under a leafy oak or take his morning dip in the thawing brook among the pines. He was no less enthusiastic in his appreciation of the historical beauty of Spanish towns and villages, and had made a detailed study of Spanish architecture. An excellent musician, he delighted in Mozart, whose refinement and delicate tenderness are indeed in harmony with his own spirit. Yet this man, who was sensitive to the slightest smile of beauty in nature and art, lived a life of the utmost simplicity, bordering on poverty. His attire had no luxury but that of scrupulous cleanliness, no art but that of an instinctive and natural elegance. He was small and thin, as if all his person had been concentrated in his beautifully expressive head—where his eyes shone with a smile not altogether devoid of a point of mischievous irony which was welcome in a face radiant with human kindness.

He never married. Yet he prized the joys of family life above all others, and the company of children was indispensable to him. He found an ideal home in the house of his favourite disciple, Don Manuel B. Cossío, the eminent art critic who has done so much to make the world appreciate the real greatness of El Greco. Here, under the shadow of the Institución which he had founded and which absorbed much of his time, Don Francisco lived long years of quiet but deep and intense action. His method was that of personal influence—the transmission of that mysterious magnetism which all great teachers possess and seem to carry in their own persons, for it does not act through the dead letter of their teachings and requires their presence and figure. Whether in his class-room at the University or at the Institución, or in the drawing-room of his house or in his frequent ramblings with friends and pupils through the hills and dales of the Sierra, Don Francisco was always the same : not a professor, not a pedagogue, but a friend, a companion, a spiritual guide, a giver of courage to the weak, of counsel to the strong, of graceful and delicate rebuke to the straying—a being, as Maeztu has admirably said of him, more flame than light.

His mind had that Socratic humility which is content to wait for truth and leave to it the care of its own defence—that humility, indeed, which comes from confidence, not in one's own mind, but in the Oneness of the mind of Nature. That was the secret of the apparent contradiction between his intellectual steadfastness and his real, not merely courteous, tolerance of other people's opinions. His method was by suggestion and stimulation, rather than by direct statement, and he often achieved by indirect example conversions which no direct argument could have brought about.

No man was ever worthier of bearing the name of the saint of Assisi. Don Francisco Giner was a true Franciscan, and his whole life was instinct with that universal love with which St. Francis enriched the spirit of the world. It is worthy of notice in this connexion that Don Francisco detected the value of Galdós at the very beginning of the career of this great novelist whose works are so deeply instilled with that sense of universal love. In this respect the few pages which Giner devoted to the study of Galdós in the early days of their public life are significant, and reveal a deep spiritual relationship between two great Spanish figures of the nineteenth century otherwise wide apart in their life-work and outlook.

Differing in this from most of the progressive men of his time in Spain, Don Francisco was fervently religious. He never belonged to any definite confession, but he lived his religion far more truly than do the immense majority of those who label their beliefs with one or other of the current labels. His soul was typically Spanish in its blend of mysticism and militancy, of action and contemplation. Indeed, he would agree with St. Teresa, or for that matter with Don Quixote himself, in the view that action and contemplation are but two aspects of one and the same thing, and that the one is of no avail without the other. Don Francisco lived up to this Golden Rule of Spanish religious life. The outward sign of this rule is a complete lack of self-seeking.

Hence, the spiritual radiance which emanated from his figure. Don Francisco stands as the source of strength for all the generations which have come of age since the closing years of the nineteenth century. Directly or indirectly, consciously or unconsciously, there is no man who counts in Spanish culture to-day who has not come under the influence of his teachings, and particularly of the highest of them—a life agitated and courageous in its youth, noble and serene in old age, and always clean, pure, and devoted to the service of man.

RAMÓN PÉREZ DE AYALA

VICTOR HUGO, who did not know Spain, though he thought he did, speaks in one of his poems of ' mes Espagnes ', in the plural. That is probably the best, or at any rate the most accurate thing he ever said about Spain. Spain is plural. Her ancient kingdoms, however much carved into artificial provinces by the theoretical constitution-builders of 1812, still live, if not in legal and official papers, yet with the more fruitful life of nature and the spirit.

Thus the genius of Spain is to-day as composite as ever, and we must expect to find in it the intensity, earnestness, and quaint lack of grace of the Basque, the intellectualism and imitative talent of the Catalan, the Mediterranean sense of eloquence and form of the Valencian, the graceful, and at times deeply significant spontaneity of the Andalusian, the dry but warm inspiration of Castile, the primitive force of Aragon, the lyrical sweetness of Galicia, and that elusive charm which makes of Asturias a kingdom apart among the kingdoms of Spain.

Asturias, the smallest of ' the Spains ', is a country which stretches as a compromise between the Cantabrian Range and the sea, linking up the two irreconcilable opposites by means of an ingenious system of valleys. Mountains, valleys, and seas, together with that soft, delicate atmosphere which such complex countries usually enjoy under moderate climates, are the formative elements of the Asturian character. And thus we find in the Asturians that noble attitude, that elevated outlook, which the eyes of mountaineers, slowly and through generations, teach their minds and hearts ; that shrewdness, that penetration, and that

psychological insight which fancy would fain attribute
to the even-present insinuating example of their
tortuous valleys ; and that generous spirit, universal
and wide as the sea, which explains why the Asturian
people excel all the other peoples of the peninsula in
political genius. Nor is this the only quality which
differentiates them from the rest of Spain. For the
softer atmosphere of their little fatherland seems to
find its counterpart in a subtlety, a sense of nuances,
a capacity for light treatment and suggestion, and
above all a sense of humour, which make of them the
most gifted of Spaniards in qualities of intellectual
distinction.

Indeed, it is not too much to say that the Asturian
character is in a sense antithetical to that of the rest
of the Spanish race. While Spain is above all creative
and excels in genius, Asturias is mostly critical, and its
distinctive gift is talent. Asturias is therefore conscious, and in this, the deepest possible sense, it
undoubtedly is the most European of the kingdoms
of Spain. True, in an external and superficial way,
Catalonia would appeal to most people as the representative, in Spain, of European civilization and
progress. This opinion we hold to be mistaken. For
the genius of Catalonia is mainly imitative and formal,
and its character is essentially conservative. Catalonia
endeavours to be like Europe. Asturias endeavours
to be fully and consciously herself, and this is more
truly European. It thus becomes clear why her men
should always have been in the van of political progress
in the Peninsula. It was in Asturias that Charles III
found his enlightened statesmen. It is from Asturias
that contemporary Spain draws her pioneers in
education, politics, and social reform. Thus Asturias,
in whose territory began the Reconquest—the reassertion of Europe over Africa and Asia in the disputed
borderlands of Spain—is still the stronghold of the

European spirit in the most Oriental of western countries.

Asturias is represented in Spanish contemporary letters by Don Ramón Pérez de Ayala, whose volume of short stories, *Prometeo*, is now available in English. Pérez de Ayala, though young, is not a beginner. Apart from the above-mentioned book, he has published seven novels,[1] three volumes of verse, and several books of criticism and essays. He is a prominent figure in contemporary Spanish letters, a shrewd critic, a keen student of English literature. Any one of these activities would justify the drawing of an outline of his literary personality.

Pérez de Ayala is a typical Asturian in the intelligent and intellectual outlook which distinguishes his writings. He is above all a cultivated man, a modern humanist, a conscious intellect with a comprehensive view of history and a serene understanding of the world and of life. His favourite attitude is that of the spectator, and, though far from indifferent to the ethical issues involved in literature and certainly not devoid of a warm feeling of human fellowship, his aim is neither to judge nor to plead, but merely to understand. His criticism is based on no preference for schools, forms of culture, nations, races, or religions. His mind is open to all the winds, equally transparent to all the rays that emanate from reality. A good European he certainly is in his wide appreciation of all the intellectual values which in the course of history have gone to the making of our old continent. But he would not be a Spaniard if he did not feel the call of Oriental thoughts and faiths, nor if his mind were insensitive to the breadth of new life which comes to Europe over the wide Western Ocean. As a critic, he is not hampered by the iron bars of

[1] Two of them published since this essay was written.

Catholic dogma which, despite his subtlety and elevation, often hindered the free movements of that great master, Menéndez y Pelayo ; but he is if anything still more free from that rationalistic turn of mind which in the nineteenth century has blighted so many excellent Spanish intellects. His taste is solidly grounded on truth and human nature, and refined by familiarity with the great European masters.

Such criticism—the true one—resolves itself into the collation of art with life, and ultimately rests on psychology. Ayala is a consummate psychologist, and he is never more fortunate than when, giving full scope to his natural proclivities, he analyses the psychological background of plays, persons, and events. Curiously enough, this detached observer of life seems to prefer to the study of motives the exploration of the obscure region where the springs of emotion are hidden. Many are the pages where with masterly hand he has set down the delicate movements of the soul tossed to and fro in the vacillating border between laughter and tears.

Observation is the basis of psychology, and Ayala is a good observer. But there is a kind of observation, more usually to be found with creative genius, which consists in a quiet, almost passive contemplation, a ' soaking-in ' of impressions half-consciously felt and absorbed by the mind. This is not Ayala's way. His observation is rather a keen and penetrating attention which owes less to the actual stimulus of reality than to the quick intellectual sensibility of a mind rich in ideas and ready to yield a generous flow of thought at the slightest provocation. Hence the peculiar character of his critical work, which is not constructed in logical fashion so much as poured out in a kind of liquid vein of ideas. This does not by any means imply that Ayala is poor in dialectical powers. Far from it. To his Asturian origin he owes a mind of excellent

steel, which the Jesuits, his masters, took great care
to sharpen, little knowing that they would be the
first to suffer from its edge,[1] and his essays and novels,
even his verse, are witness that he loves an argument
as much as any Scot.   But it is not the dialectic mind
that is the most logically constructive, and Ayala
seems to prefer for his critical work the fluid atmosphere
of the English *essay* to the clear-cut plan of the French
étude.   It may be that, to a certain extent, this fluid
impression which his essays give, as if he had been
thinking aloud before a shorthand typist, may be due
to the hurried way in which nowadays the newspaper
forces the critic to work for an impatient public used
to breakfasting with ideas.   Many, if not all, of
Ayala's essays were written as press reviews.   A certain
inequality in his style, usually good, sometimes rising
to a high level of expressiveness, but at times bald and
bare, suggest a work written without that preparation
in still leisure which alone can give unity of texture
to substance and form.   But there is something deeper
than mere hurry in his manner.   There is an intellectual attitude.   Ayala does not look at his subject from
the ground of a fundamental principle.   His view of
life and the world is too complex, and perhaps too
detached also ; and thus he prefers to look at his
subject very much as a collector looks at a small
objet d'art, this way and that, and this way again, in
every possible light.

It is perhaps in his poetry that Ayala gives the clearest
exposition of his philosophy and of his creed.   This
poetry is so far represented by three volumes (two
of which, the first and the second, are now issued
together), bearing names which suggest a certain
sequence : *La Paz del Sendero, El Sendero Innumerable,
El Sendero Andante*.   The uniformity of the titles does

[1] *A. M. D. G.*, a novel by R. Pérez de Ayala.

not, however, correspond to any continuity in treatment or in outer subject, though the recurrence of the
word *sendero*, path, does convey the idea of self-
development along the road of experience which is
the real inner subject of all. The first volume, *La Paz
del Sendero*, appeared in 1903, ushered in by no less
a preface-writer than Rubén Darío. Despite its display
of almost peasant-like simplicity, this work betrays
the intellectual reader of home and foreign poetry.
Thus, the opening poem, that which gives its title
to the book, is an admirable adaptation to modern
uses of the mediaeval stanza known in Spanish literature as *cuaderna vía*. We note here a merely formal
reminiscence of Juan Ruiz, the Archpriest of Hita,
in more ways than one, as we shall have to observe
anon, a literary ancestor of Ayala. Together with the
revival of this national vein, Ayala's early poems show
a strong subservience to the poetical manner of Francis
Jammes. This is clear in Ayala's attitude towards old
houses, animals, and nature, and it goes as far as close
imitation in the following passage :

Aquí en mi casa de campo,
tengo una vieja butaca

de gutapercha ; y es tan

humilde la pobre anciana
que cuando algun visi-
    tante
viene a verme, no repara

en ella, y me dice :—Siempre
tan solo, señor Ayala.
¿ No se aburre sin salir ?

Y yo pienso cuando
    marcha
que las gentes son muy
    frívolas,

Il y a une armoire à peine luisante
Qui a entendu les voix de mes
    grand'tantes,
Qui a entendu la voix de mon
    grand-père,
Qui a entendu la voix de mon père.
À ces souvenirs l'armoire est fidèle,
On a tort de croire qu'elle ne sait
    que se taire,
Car je cause avec elle.

·   ·   ·   ·

Il est venu chez moi bien des
    hommes et des femmes
Qui n'ont pas crû à ces petites
    âmes.
Et je souris que l'on me pense seul
    vivant

muy soberbias y muy vanas	Quand un visiteur me dit en entrant :
porque no miran siquiera a esta valetudinaria.[1]	— Comment allez-vous, Monsieur Jammes ?

This close imitation of Francis Jammes suggests more than one feature of Ayala's poetry. Quaintness and tenderness are two well-known characteristics of the Asturian nature. They are conspicuous in Francis Jammes's work and easily explain why it should have had in France at the time a *succès de nouveauté*. Led away by this instinctive sympathy between his own nature and that which in the French poet was at most a *manner* of the mind, Ayala does not seem to have been able to avoid in some of the poems of this first book the pitfall towards which Francis Jammes himself had strayed—a certain affectation which is the weak point of a poetry otherwise not devoid of a peculiar charm. But, though as an imitator of Jammes Ayala naturally proved inferior to his model, the youthful Asturian poet already revealed in some compositions of this his early work an earnestness which was to prove his salvation—an earnestness in which it was possible to detect two wholly different moods : one dominated by a philosophical, almost religious preoccupation with the idea of destiny : the other, marked by an æsthetic instinct towards truth and restrained expression. Hence, despite a certain awkwardness which is not without an attractiveness of its own, a work full of beauty in which the typical qualities of Ayala's style can already be detected : his rich vocabulary, his sense of the value and the music of words, his

---

[1] Here in my country house I have an old arm-chair, and so old and so humble, the poor old friend, that when visitors come to see me they do not notice her, and say : ' Always alone, Señor Ayala ! Don't you get bored at home ? ' And when they go, I muse how frivolous people are, how conceited and how vain, for they will not even look at my valetudinary friend.

precision, his clear vision and the neatness of his expression.   These qualities appear at their best when Ayala describes those fugitive movements of nature which are so tempting a material for the artist :

> . . . el cielo que en dedos de diamante
> hila sutiles hilos de lluvia en sus mil ruecas. . . .[1]

> Sobre el lago del cielo arrojaron la luna
> y su claror plateado difundiendo va una
> melodía de halos, que son como aureolas
> crecientes, en un ritmo ondulante de olas.[2]

These are good beginnings for a poet.   But still better is the strength which can rise to the beautiful simplicity of

> Divino peregrino,
> mi pensamiento sigue ese blanco camino.[3]

'Mi pensamiento.'   Observe the word.   Poetry, said Wordsworth, is an overflow of emotion with an undercurrent of thought.   Ayala's poetry would be more accurately described as a flow of thought with an undercurrent of emotion, and, though in his early work there is a youthful generosity of feeling which the more mature poet will carefully restrain, it is already possible to detect in it both the strength and the weakness inherent in such an inverted kind of poetry.   To his earnest nature Ayala owes his freedom from rhetoric.   Coming after the period when Spanish poets seemed to be taking refuge in a rhetoric of passion from the merely verbal rhetoric of their predecessors, Ayala's subdued emotions and penetrating ideas,

[1]   . . . the sky with diamond fingers
Spins subtle threads of rain on a thousand wheels. . . .

[2]   On the lake of the sky the moon was thrown
And its silvery gleam diffuses on its way
A melody of halos like aureolas growing
Ever wider with the undulating rhythm of waves.

[3]   A divine pilgrim,
My thought walks on this white road.

appearing in a closely fitting verbal garment, gracefully but sparingly decorated, brought to Spanish poetry precisely that kind of progress which was to be expected from the well-balanced genius of Asturias. His main weakness lies perhaps in a tendency to sink into mere criticism. True poetry can only be written when emotion is duly ballasted with thought, but too much thought, or too little emotion, may prevent the soaring of poetry. The critic in Ayala often pulls down the poet. His poetry then falls into the anecdotical, the didactical, or merely the jocular. This feature, curiously enough, is not so prominent in his early as in his later work.

Not that Ayala's powers as a poet are diminished by time. Far from it. *El Sendero Innumerable,* which follows *La Paz del Sendero* after an interval of twelve years, abounds in excellent verse, and contains perhaps two or three pages of the best contemporary Spanish poetry. Nothing so satisfactorily complete, so deeply philosophical, and so truly poetical as the pages in which Ayala has interpreted the many souls and the one soul of the sea—a symbol of the many souls and the one soul of man and the world—nothing so earnest and so beautiful, so ample, and so minutely exact, has probably been written in modern Spanish verse. In these pages, Ayala finds his true self as the poet of intellectual emotion. The sea, with its unity and its variety, seems to inspire this, his highest poetical mood, with particular felicity. For it is again in a sea-poem that he reaches his best in his third volume, *El Sendero Andante.* Only here, in *El Niño en la Playa,* Ayala is even more completely himself. For, along with that wealth of philosophical meaning which makes him look at nature with eyes full of the spirit of man ; along with his genius for the rhythmical interpretation of natural movements and his sensibility to colours, scents, sounds, and tastes, we find again the generous

emotion of his youth, well under control, yet warm
with the deepest of Spanish affections, the love of the
child ; and that Asturian tenderness—here free from
all quaintness and affectation—which delights in meek
animals ; his skilful use of old Spanish verse-forms,
and even that ethical turn of mind which must arm
the poem with a didactical point, yet does it with so
light a touch, so elusive a grace, that the poetic value
of the whole, far from suffering, is enhanced.

' The struggle to apprehend the supernal Loveli-
ness—this struggle, on the part of souls fittingly
constituted—has given to the world all *that* which it
(the world) has ever been enabled at once to understand and to *feel* as poetic.' This quotation from
Edgar Allan Poe appears in English at the head of
La Paz del Sendero. It is a significant declaration of
principle to which our poet has been loyal with
singular consistency. The words of Poe make it clear
why Ayala should be above all a poet of intellectual
emotion, a poet, that is, who seeks to quicken his own
perception of nature while respecting nature's independent existence, refraining, therefore, from colouring
her with his own subjective moods and trusting that
emotion will rise from the innate harmony between
the world and man—man, of course, endowed with the
vision and the faculty divine. Shelley was such a poet.
But Shelley's way of poetically understanding nature
resolved itself into animating the ideas of natural
things, giving them a motion, a character, and an
expression all their own (or maybe, Shelley's own).
Shelley, however, was an English Platonist ; while
Ayala is Spanish, that is, he belongs to a race whose
natural bent it is to consider man as the centre of
things. His way, therefore, of poetically understanding nature consists rather in discovering in
nature the human—not man's ephemeral moods and
feelings, but the permanently and universally human

which is Man. This obviously leads to the identifica-
tion of man and nature as two different forms of one
and the same life. All is one and the same. This
conclusion, the natural outcome of such an attitude
of mind, is expressed in the last poem *Filosofía*, in
Ayala's latest volume. It is a poem in which the idea
is developed with the skill, finesse, and rhythmical
elegance which our poet so easily reaches under his
intellectual inspiration.

Whenever the Spanish mind has been free from the
overgrowth of dogmatic doctrines—whether religious
or philosophical—which often cover its natural form,
it has settled down to this attitude, ultimately panthe-
istic perhaps, but primarily ' pan-human '. It is the
secret of that æsthetic impartiality which is the mark
of the old-time Spanish classics, from the epics of
Myo Cid to the versified ramblings through experience
which we owe to Juan Ruiz of Hita. In Ayala, this
feeling of human fellowship is so genuine that he can
strike the classical tone without effort by merely letting
his creative spirit, moved by true humanism, follow
the dictates of an unfailing literary taste. A style
results which, in his later works of fiction at least,
is perhaps the most truly, most elegantly, yet most
freely Spanish style of our generation.
It is a constant feature of Spanish classics that they
deal with man pre-eminently as an individual, so that
they are often led to situations of a character, conventionally at least if not essentially, anti-social.
Adventurers, rogues, prostitutes, often considered in
other literatures as merely picturesque material, are,
for that deeper and more human reason, favourite
subjects of Spanish art. Ayala is no exception to this
rule, and disreputable folk occupy a considerable place
in his fiction. Even in his early work, he has handled
this difficult material, if not always with sure taste,

at least often with singular good fortune ; witness that interesting chapter in *Troteras y Danzaderas,* in which a young and cultivated artist reads Shakespeare's *Othello* to a wholly illiterate girl, rich only in the wisdom of the streets, and delights in her spontaneous reactions as the tragedy reveals itself to the young woman. These four first novels, *Tinieblas en las Cumbres, A. M. D. G., La Pata de la Raposa,* and *Troteras y Danzaderas* (a title, this last one, which savours of Juan Ruiz), are but the steps by which the novelist rises to his full stature. The raw matter of the author's experience appears in them as yet insufficiently wrought out by art. Yet the gradation of progress is obvious as we pass from the first to the last of them, and constitutes a striking proof of the consistency and the continuity of Ayala's development. But it is in the *Novelas Poemáticas,* of which an English translation is available, that Ayala reveals himself as a complete artist of fiction. Here at last we have a modern mind, conscious of his links with a racial past which manifests itself in continuity of spiritual and formal traditions, whose powers of observation are enriched by the habit of dwelling on the eternal questionings of man, and whose powers of expression are rendered more telling and subtle by a poetical mind, skilled in the use of symbols. These three short stories are little masterpieces of observation, of original creation and arrangement, of truly poetical feeling and of smiling humour, despite their inexorable Spanish realism. *Prometeo,* in particular, the first of them, is written on a level of gentle irony so delicately defined that even its desolate end cannot destroy the elusive charm of the tale, while its composition, with its admirable adaptation of mythological language to the life of present-day Spain, is so ample and free, so deeply human despite its strictly logical and intellectual substratum, as to make of this

story a real apologue, a true *enxienplo*, in the manner
of Don Juan Manuel, with the added merit of beauty.

The *Novelas Poemáticas* offer numerous cases of that
perfect adaptation of form to substance which is the
essence of *style*, the style of great writers, not of mere
stylists. Such is, for instance, the opening of *Prometeo*.
There are passages in this book written with so true
a sense of language that they sound to the mind's ear
like an echo of the voice of Cervantes. But pray do
not imagine that this high level of writing is—or can
be—reached by endeavouring to raise the tone to the
classic pitch, by donning as it were the Spanish six-
teenth-century ruff. It is sheer directness and
simplicity, together with the right human attitude,
which makes the following lines sound like a reminiscence of immortal words :

> Odysseus deseaba partirse, y no sabía cómo, que Federica
> no le retuviese con llantos, clamores y escándalo. Por
> olvidarse de su congoja, y con achaque de que gustaba
> mucho de la natación, Odysseus se pasaba casi todo el día
> en el mar. Nadaba como un tritón. Ibase mar adentro,
> y se estaba cuatro y cinco horas nadando sin cesar. Y,
> cuando no estaba en el baño, procuraba acogerse a la esqui-
> vidad de un bosque, en donde suspiraba largamente por su
> libertad perdida. Hasta que se determinó en su ánimo
> a escapar. Y fué de esta suerte . . .[1]

Thus in full possession of his instrument, Ayala
might well attempt the writing of a full-fledged novel.
Such a novel, and no ordinary one, he has given us in
his *Belarmino y Apolonio*. In a sense, one might con-

---

[1] Odysseus wanted to depart, and knew not how, so that Federica
should not retain him with tears, plaints and outcry. Seeking to
forget his anguish, and under cover of his love of swimming, Odysseus
spent most of the day in the water. He swam like a Triton. He
went far out to sea and remained four and five hours swimming
unceasingly. And, when not bathing, he sought protection in the
seclusion of a forest, where long he sighed for his lost liberty. Till
finally he made up his mind to escape. And it was in this guise . . .

sider this book as a dialectic illustration of the theme
treated in the little poem *Filosofía* : *All is one and the
same*. Belarmino, the shoemaker philosopher, in
search of a word which will express all the ideas of man,
and Apolonio, the shoemaker poet-dramatist, in search
of glory and the majesty of an attitude, may well stand
for two opposite principles, two types : the one, eager
to understand, the other eager to express ; the one
sensitive yet calm, the other interested, yet insensitive.
Fortunately, however, these two types are animated
with a really individual life which makes of them men
of so original and vivid a character that, though in so
far as it concerns them the novel is not particularly
rich in action, the story is brimful of human interest
and sympathy, and we close the book with regret, as
one parts with friends. Ayala has embroidered a love-
tale into the loose canvas of an artistic rivalry between
the two intellectual cobblers. Baldly told, this tale of
a young seminarist—the son of Apolonio—who elopes
with the niece and adopted daughter of Belarmino, is
compelled by a kind but bullying benefactress to
abandon the girl, and, when a priest, finds her again
and saves her from the abyss of degradation into which
she had fallen, contains humorous possibilities of
deplorable romance. That Ayala has avoided every
single one of the many pitfalls on his path is not
enough, for that was to be expected of his mature
taste. But he has drawn his story with a hand so sure
and firm, yet so light, in a mood so humorous and
detached, yet so moving, that what seemed to be ill-
chosen material turns out to be the basis for his
triumph as an artist—never more skilful than in what
he leaves out.

In this mature piece of work Ayala's main characteristics as a creative artist appear mellowed and combined. That tendency to look at the object from
different angles, which in his critical work resulted in
a somewhat vacillating arrangement, develops here into

an original system of composition which presents the
story now acted and in the present, now told and in
the past, seen now by one or other of the protagonists,
now by the author, now directly by the reader—and all
these different perspectives perfectly harmonized.
That flow of ideas which we noticed as typical of
Ayala's work, appear here as abundant as ever, perhaps
we might say a little too abundant, but ordered and
canalized and admirably distributed amongst the
most intellectual actors in the novel according to
their particular natures. The poetical turn of mind
of the author is obvious in the spirit which pervades the
work. This poetical spirit seems to intensify the human
sympathy with which all the characters are treated—
a human sympathy exquisitely blended with humour
and a keen sense of the comic—in the true Spanish
vein. Ayala can love with a smile. It is again this
poetic undercurrent which enables him delicately to
emphasize the importance which he attaches to sex.
The sensuous element in man and nature is a favourite
thread in Ayala's discourse, a thread finely spun, with
a neatness and a classical pulchritude typified in his
frequent use of the adjective *venusto*. The differences
in the quantity and quality of sensuousness in his
characters are a striking sign of the discrimination and
care with which he treats this all-important aspect of
nature. Such types as the French pastrycook, Monsieur Colignon, bursting with *joie de vivre*, and the
old maid Felicita Quemada, consumed with sup-
pressed passion, are admirably observed and rendered,
and the contrast is significant between the inflamma-
bility of Apolonio, the cobbler-dramatist, and the utter
lack of sensuousness in Belarmino, the cobbler-
philosopher.

This feature of Ayala's art contributes not a little
to enhance the peculiar charm of his treatment of
landscape. We all know that *un paysage est un état
d'âme*, but few of us can apply the dictum to our art.

Ayala succeeds here and there in giving us that sense of being before a moment of nature, and his success is often due to the boldness with which he

> dared uplift
> The closest, all-concealing tunic

of nature.

Era la sazón otoñal, de color de miel y niebla aterciopelada y argentina, a manera de vello, con que la tierra estaba como un melocotón maduro. Por encima de las tapias del huerto conventual asomaban los negros y rígidos cipreses, que eran como el prólogo del arrobo místico, el dechado de la voluntad eréctil y aspiración al trance ; y los sauces anémicos y adolecientes — en la región los llaman desmayos — , que eran la fatiga y rendimiento, epílogo dulce del místico espasmo ; y los pomares sinuosos y musculosos, las ramas, de agarrotados dedos, mostrando rojas y pequeñas manzanas, que no sugerían la imagen del pecado, sino a lo más, de un pecadillo. Para los ojos, todo era paz en el huerto conventual ; para el oído, la querellosa algarabía de los gorriones vespertinos.[1]

Such examples of acute penetration are frequent in Ayala's later work. They reveal a personality calm and detached in outward appearance, yet deeply sensitive to the inner currents of sympathy between man and the world. ' The philosopher '—says the famished student Aligator in *Belarmino y Apolonio*— ' is the inverse type of the dramatist. Outwardly, all serenity and impassiveness ; in his most secret self, inextinguishable ardour.' Aligator wrote these words thinking of Belarmino. We might perhaps apply them to Ayala himself.

[1] It was the autumn season, with its colour like honey and its velvety and silvery mist, like bloom, so that the earth seemed a ripe peach. Over the walls of the convent garden rose the black and rigid cypresses which were like the prologue of the mystical rapture, the symbol of taut will and of the aspiration to the trance ; and the anæmic, suffering willows,—*dismays* is their local name—which were like the fatigue and exhaustion, the sweet epilogue of the mystic spasm ; and the sinuous and muscular apple-trees, whose knotty-fingered branches did not suggest the image of sin, but at most, of peccadilloes. For the eyes, all was peace in the garden of the convent ; for the ears, the quarrelsome hullabaloo raised by the evening sparrows.

MIGUEL DE UNAMUNO

I sat, several years ago, at the Welsh National Eisteddfod, under the vast tent in which the Bard of Wales was being crowned. After the small golden crown had been placed in unsteady equilibrium on the head of a clever-looking pressman, several Welsh bards came on the platform and recited little epigrams. A Welsh bard is, if young, a pressman, and if of maturer years, a divine. In this case, as England was at war, they were all of the maturer kind, and, while I listened to the music of their ditties—the sense thereof being, alas! beyond my reach—I was struck by the fact that all of them, though different, closely resembled Don Miguel de Unamuno. It is not my purpose to enter into the wasp-nest of racial disquisitions. If there is a race in the world over which more sense and more nonsense can be freely said, for lack of definite information, than the Welsh, it is surely this ancient Basque people, whose greatest contemporary figure is perhaps Don Miguel de Unamuno. I am merely setting down that intuitional fact for what it may be worth, though I do not hide my opinion that such promptings of the inner, untutored man are worth more than cavefuls of bones and tombfuls of undecipherable papers.

This reminiscence, moreover, which springs up into the light of my memory every time I think of Don Miguel de Unamuno, has to my mind a further value in that in it the image of Don Miguel does not appear as evoked by one man, but by many, though many of one species, many who in depth are but one man, one type, the Welsh divine. Now, this unity underlying a multiplicity, these many faces, moods, and movements, traceable to one only type, I find deeply connected in my mind with Unamuno's person and with what he signifies in Spanish life and letters. And when I further delve into my impression, I first realize an undoubtedly physical relation between the many-one Welsh divines and the many-one Unamuno. A tall, broad-shouldered, bony man, with high cheeks, a beak-like nose, pointed grey beard, and a complexion the colour of the red hæmatites on which Bilbao, his native town, is built, and which Bilbao ruthlessly plucks from its very body to exchange for gold in the markets of England—and in the deep sockets under the high aggressive forehead prolonged by short iron-grey hair, two eyes like gimlets eagerly watching the world through spectacles which seem to be purposely pointed at the object like microscopes ; a fighting expression, but of noble fighting, above the prizes of the passing world, the contempt for which is shown in a peculiar attire whose blackness invades even that little triangle of white which worldly men leave on their breast for the necktie of frivolity and the decorations of vanity, and, blinding it, leaves but the thinnest rim of white collar to emphasize, rather than relieve, the priestly effect of the whole. Such is Don Miguel de Unamuno.

Such is, rather, his photograph. For Unamuno himself is ever changing. A talker, as all good Spaniards are nowadays, but a talker in earnest and with his heart in it, he is varied, like the subjects of his conversation, and, still more, like the passions which they awake in him. And here I find an unsought reason in intellectual support of that intuitional observation which I noted down in starting—that Unamuno resembles the Welsh in that he is not ashamed of showing his passions—a thing which he has often to do, for he is very much alive and feels therefore plenty of them. But a word of caution may here be necessary, since that term, ' passion ', having been diminished—that is, made meaner—by the world, an erroneous impression might be conveyed by what precedes, of the life and ways of Unamuno. So that it may not be superfluous to say that Don Miguel de Unamuno is a Professor of Greek in the University of Salamanca, an ex-Rector of it who left behind the reputation of being a strong ruler; a father of a numerous family, and a man who has sung the quiet and deep joys of married life with a restraint, a vigour, and a nobility which it would be difficult to match in any literature. *Yet* a passionate man—or, as he would perhaps prefer to say, *therefore* a passionate man. But in a major, not in a minor key; of strong, not of weak, passions.

The difference between the two lies perhaps in that the man with strong passions lives them, while the man with weak passions is lived by them, so that while weak passions paralyse the will, strong passions urge man to action. It is such an urge towards life, such a vitality ever awake, which inspires Unamuno's multifarious activities in the realm of the mind. The duties of his chair of Greek are the first claim upon his time. But then, his reading is prodigious. Not only is he familiar with the stock-in-trade of every intellectual worker—the Biblical, Greek, Roman, and Italian cultures—but there is hardly anything worth reading in Europe and America which he has not read, and, but for the Slav languages, in the original. Though never out of Spain, and seldom out of Salamanca, he has succeeded in establishing direct connexions with most of the intellectual leaders of the world, and in gathering an astonishingly accurate knowledge of the spirit and literature of foreign peoples. It was in his library at Salamanca that he once explained to an Englishman the meaning of a particular Scotticism in Robert Burns, and it was there that he congratulated another Englishman on his having read *Rural Rides*, ' the hall-mark ', he said, ' of the man of letters who is no mere man of letters, but also a man '. From that corner of Castile, he has poured out his spirit in essays, poetry, criticism, novels, philosophy, lectures, and public meetings, and that daily toil of press-article writing which is the duty rather than the privilege of most present-day writers in Spain. Such are the many faces, moods, and movements in which Unamuno appears before Spain and the world. And yet, despite this multiplicity and this dispersion, the dominant impression which his personality leaves behind is that of a vigorous unity, an unswerving concentration both of mind and purpose. Bagaria, the national caricaturist, a genius of rhythm and character which the war revealed, but who was too good not to be overshadowed by the facile art of Raemaekers (imagine Goya over-shadowed by Reynolds !), once represented Unamuno as an owl. A marvellous thrust at the heart of Unamuno's character. For all this vitality and ever-moving activity of mind is shot through by the absolute immobility of two owlish eyes piercing the darkness of spiritual night. And this intense gaze into the mystery is the steel axis round which his spirit revolves and revolves in desperation ; the unity under his multiplicity ; the one fire under his passions and the inspiration of his whole work and life.

It was Unamuno himself who once said that the Basque is the alkaloid of the Spaniard. The saying is true, so far as it goes. But it would be more accurate to say ' one of the two alkaloids '. It is probable that if the Spanish character were analysed—always provided that the Mediterranean aspect of it be left aside as a thing apart—two main principles would be recognized in it, i.e. the Basque, richer in concentration, substance, strength ; and the Andalusian, more given to observation, grace, form. The two types are to this day socially opposed. The Andalusian is a people which has lived down many civilizations, and in which even illiterate peasants possess a kind of innate education. The Basques are a primitive people of mountaineers and fishermen, in which even scholars have a peasant-like roughness not unlike the roughness of Scotch tweeds—or character. It is the even balancing of these two elements—the force of the Northerner with the grace of the Southerner—which gives the Castilian his admirable poise and explains the graceful virility of men such as Fray Luis de León and the feminine strength of women such as Queen Isabel and Santa Teresa. We are therefore led to expect in so forcible a representative of the Basque race as Unamuno the more substantial and earnest features of the Spanish spirit.

Our expectation is not disappointed. And to begin with it appears in that very concentration of his mind and soul on the mystery of man's destiny on earth. Unamuno is in earnest, in dead earnest, as to this matter. This earnestness is a distinct Spanish, nay, Basque feature in him. There is something of the stern attitude of Loyola about his ' tragic sense of life ', and on this subject—under one form or another, his only subject—he admits no joke, no flippancy, no subterfuge. A true heir of those great Spanish saints and mystics whose lifework was devoted to the exploration of the kingdoms of faith, he is more human than they in that he has lost hold of the firm ground where they had stuck their anchor. Yet though loose in the modern world, he refuses to be drawn away from the main business of the Christian, the saving of his soul, which, in his interpretation, means the conquest of his immortality, his own immortality.

An individualist. Certainly. And he proudly claims the title. Nothing more refreshing in these days of hoggish communistic cant than this great voice asserting the divine, the eternal rights of the individual.

But it is not with political rights that he is concerned. Political individualism, when not a mere blind for the unlimited freedom of civil privateering, is but the outcome of that abstract idea of man which he so energetically condemns as pedantic—that is, inhuman. His opposition of the individual to society is not that of a puerile anarchist to a no less puerile socialist. There is nothing childish about Unamuno. His assertion that society is for the individual, not the individual for society, is made on a transcendental plane. It is not the argument of liberty against authority—which can be easily answered on the rationalistic plane by showing that authority is in its turn the liberty of the social or collective being, a higher, more complex, and longer-living ' individual ' than the individual pure and simple. It is rather the unanswerable argument of eternity against duration. Now that argument must rest on a religious basis. And it is on a religious basis that Unamuno founds his individualism. Hence the true Spanish flavour of his social theory, which will not allow itself to be set down and analysed into principles of ethics and politics, with their inevitable tendency to degenerate into mere economics, but remains free and fluid and absolute, like the spirit.

Such an individualism has therefore none of the features of that childish half-thinking which inspires most anarchists. It is, on the contrary, based on high thinking, the highest of all, that which refuses to dwell on anything less than man's origin and destination. We are here confronted with that humanistic tendency of the Spanish mind which can be observed as the dominant feature of her arts and literature. All races are of course predominantly concerned with man. But they all manifest their concern with a difference. Man is in Spain a concrete being, the man of flesh and bones, and the whole man. He is neither subtilized

into an idea by pure thinking nor civilized into a gentleman by social laws and prejudices. Spanish art and
letters deal with concrete, tangible persons. Now,
there is no more concrete, no more tangible person for
every one of us than ourself. Unamuno is therefore
right in the line of Spanish tradition in dealing predominantly—one might almost say always—with his
own person. The feeling of the awareness of one's
own personality has seldom been more forcibly
expressed than by Unamuno. This is primarily due to
the fact that he is himself obsessed by it. But in his
expression of it Unamuno derives also some strength
from his own sense of matter and the material—again
a typically Spanish element of his character. Thus
his human beings are as much body as soul, or rather
body and soul all in one, a union which he admirably
renders by bold mixtures of physical and spiritual
metaphors, as in *gozarse uno la carne del alma* (to enjoy
the flesh of one's own soul).

In fact, Unamuno, as a true Spaniard which he is,
refuses to surrender life to ideas, and that is why he
runs shy of abstractions, in which he sees but shrouds
wherewith we cover dead thoughts. He is solely
concerned with his own life, nothing but his life,
and the whole of his life. An egotistical position?
Perhaps. Unamuno, however, can and does answer
the charge. We can only know and feel humanity in
the one human being which we have at hand. It is by
penetrating deep into ourselves that we find our
brothers in us—branches of the same trunk which can
only touch each other by seeking their common origin.
This searching within, Unamuno has undertaken with
a sincerity, a fearlessness which cannot be excelled.
Nowhere will the reader find the inner contradictions
of a modern human being, who is at the same time
healthy and capable of thought, set down with a
greater respect for truth. Here the uncompromising

tendency of the Spanish race, whose eyes never turn away from nature, however unwelcome the sight, is strengthened by that passion for life which burns in Unamuno. The suppression of the slightest thought or feeling for the sake of intellectual order would appeal to him as a despicable worldly trick. Thus it is precisely because he does sincerely feel a passionate love of his own life that he thinks out with such scrupulous accuracy every argument which he finds in his mind—his own mind, a part of his life—against the possibility of life after death ; but it is also because he feels that, despite such conclusive arguments, his will to live perseveres, that he refuses to his intellect the power to kill his faith. A knight-errant of the spirit, as he himself calls the Spanish mystics, he starts for his adventures after having, like Hernán Cortés, burnt his ships. But, is it necessary to enhance his figure by literary comparison ? He is what he wants to be, a man—in the striking expression which he chose as a title for one of his short stories, *nothing less than a whole man.* Not a mere thinking machine, set to prove a theory, nor an actor on the world stage, singing a well-built poem, well built at the price of many a compromise ; but a whole man, with all his affirmations and all his negations, all the pitiless thoughts of a penetrating mind that denies, and all the desperate self-assertions of a soul that yearns for eternal life.

This strife between enemy truths, the truth thought and the truth felt, or, as he himself puts it, between veracity and sincerity, is Unamuno's *raison d'être.* And it is because the *Tragic Sense of Life* is the most direct expression of it that this book is his masterpiece. The conflict is here seen as reflected in the person of the author. The book opens by a definition of the Spanish man, the ' man of flesh and bones ', illustrated by the consideration of the real living men who stood behind the bookish figures of great philosophers and consciously or unconsciously shaped and misshaped their doctrines in order to satisfy their own vital yearnings. This is followed by the statement of the will to live or hunger for immortality, in the course of which the usual subterfuges with which this all-important issue is evaded in philosophy, theology, or mystic literature, are exposed, and the real, concrete, ' flesh and bones ' character of the immortality which men desire is reaffirmed. The Catholic position is then explained as the *vital* attitude in the matter, summed up in Tertullian's *Credo quia absurdum*, and this is opposed to the critical attitude which denies the possibility of individual survival in the sense previously defined. Thus Unamuno leads us to his inner dead-lock : his reason can rise no higher than scepticism, and, unable to become vital, dies sterile ; his faith, exacting anti-rational affirmations and unable there-fore to be apprehended by the logical mind, remains incommunicable. From the bottom of this abyss Unamuno builds up his theory of life. But is it a theory ? Unamuno does not claim for it such an intellectual dignity. He knows too well that in the constructive part of his book his vital self takes the leading part and repeatedly warns his reader of the fact, lest critical objections might be raised against this or that assumption or self-contradiction. It is on the survival of his will to live, after all the onslaughts of his critical intellect, that he finds the basis for his belief—or rather for his effort to believe. Self-compass on leads to self-love, and this self-love, founded as it is on a universal conflict, widens into love of all that lives and therefore wants to survive. So, by an act of love, springing from our own hunger for immortality, we are led to give a conscience to the Universe—that is, to create God.

Such is the process by which Unamuno, from the

transcendental pessimism of his inner contradiction, extracts an everyday optimism founded on love. His symbol of this attitude is the figure of Don Quixote, of whom he truly says that his creed ' can hardly be called idealism, since he did not fight for ideas : it was spiritualism, for he fought for the spirit '. Thus he opposes a synthetical to an analytical attitude ; a religious to an ethico-scientific ideal ; Spain, his Spain, i.e. the spiritual manifestation of the Spanish race, to Europe, his Europe, i.e. the intellectual manifestation of the white race, which he sees in Franco-Germany ; and heroic love, even when comically unpractical, to culture, which, in this book, written in 1912, is already prophetically spelt Kultura.

This courageous work is written in a style which is the man—for Buffon's saying, seldom true, applies here to the letter. It is written as Carlyle wrote, not merely with the brain, but with the whole soul and the whole body of the man, and in such a vivid manner that one can without much effort imagine the eager gesticula-tion which now and then underlines, interprets, despises, argues, denies, and above all asserts. In his absolute subservience to the matter in hand this manner of writing has its great precedent in Santa Teresa. The differences, and they are considerable, are not of art, absent in either case, but of nature. They are such deep and obvious differences as obtain between the devout, ignorant, graceful nun of six-teenth-century Avila and the free-thinking, learned, wilful professor of twentieth-century Salamanca. In the one case, as in the other, the language is the most direct and simple required. It is also the least literary and the most popular. Unamuno, who lives in close touch with the people, has enriched the Spanish literary language by returning to it many a popular term. His vocabulary abounds in words racy of the soil, and his writings gain from them an almost peasant-like pith and directness which suits his own Basque primitive nature. His expression occurs simultaneously with the thoughts and feelings to be expressed, the flow of which, but loosely controlled by the critical mind, often breaks through the meshes of established diction and gives birth to new forms created under the pressure of the moment. This feature Unamuno has also in common with Santa Teresa, but what in the Saint was a self-ignorant charm becomes in Unamuno a deliberate manner inspired, partly by an acute sense of the symbolical and psychological value of word-connexions, partly by that genuine need for expansion of the language which all true original thinkers or ' feelers ' must experience, but partly also by an acquired habit of juggling with words which is but natural in a philologist endowed with a vigorous imagination. Unamuno revels in words. He positively enjoys stretching them beyond their usual meaning, twisting them, composing, opposing, and transposing them in all sorts of possible ways. This game—not wholly unrewarded now and then by striking intellectual finds—seems to be the only relaxation which he allows his usually austere mind. It certainly is the only light feature of a style the merit of which lies in its being the close-fitting expression of a great mind earnestly concentrated on a great idea.

The earnestness, the intensity, and the oneness of his predominant passion are the main cause of the strength of Unamuno's philosophic work. They remain his main asset, yet become also the principal cause of his weakness, as a creative artist. Great art can only flourish in the temperate zone of the passions, on the return journey from the torrid. Unamuno, as a creator, has none of the failings of those artists who have never felt deeply. But he does show the

limitations of those artists who cannot cool down.
And the most striking of them is that at bottom he is
seldom able to put himself in a purely æsthetical
mood. In this, as in many other features, Unamuno
curiously resembles Wordsworth—whom, by the way,
he is one of the few Spaniards to read and appreciate.[1]
Like him, Unamuno is an essentially purposeful and
utilitarian mind. Of the two qualities which the work
of art requires for its inception—earnestness and
detachment—both Unamuno and Wordsworth possess
the first ; both are deficient in the second. Their
interest in their respective leading thought—survival
in the first, virtue in the second—is too direct, too
pressing, to allow them the ' distance ' necessary for
artistic work. Both are urged to work by a lofty
utilitarianism—the search for God through the
individual soul in Unamuno, the search for God
through the social soul in Wordsworth—so that their
thoughts and sensations are polarized and their spirit
loses that impartial transparence for nature's lights
without which no great art is possible. Once suggested, this parallel is too rich in sidelights to be lightly
dropped. This single-mindedness which distinguishes
them explains that both should have consciously or
unconsciously chosen a life of semi-seclusion, for
Unamuno lives in Salamanca very much as Wordsworth lived in the Lake District,

> in a still retreat
> Sheltered, but not to social duties lost,

hence in both a certain proclivity towards ploughing
a solitary furrow and becoming self-centred. There
are no doubt important differences. The English-

---

[1] In what follows, I confess to refer not so much to the generally
admitted opinion on Wordsworth as to my own views on him and his
poetry, which I tried to explain in my essay, ' The Case of Wordsworth ' (*Shelley and Calderon, and other Essays*, Constable & Co., 1920).

man's sense of nature is both keener and more concrete; while the Spaniard's knowledge of human
nature is not barred by the subtle inhibitions and
innate limitations which tend to blind its more unpleasant aspects to the eye of the Englishman. There
is more courage and passion in the Spaniard; more
harmony and goodwill in the Englishman; the one is
more like fire, the other like light. For Wordsworth,
a poem is above all an essay, a means for conveying
a lesson in forcible and easily remembered terms to
those who are in need of improvement. For Unamuno,
a poem or a novel (and he holds that a novel is but
a poem) is the outpouring of a man's passion, the overflow of the heart which cannot help itself and lets go.
And it may be that the essential difference between
the two is to be found in this difference between
their respective purposes: Unamuno's purpose is
more intimately personal and individual; Wordsworth's is more social and objective. Thus both miss
the temperate zone, where emotion takes shape into
the moulds of art; but while Wordsworth is driven
by his ideal of social service this side of it, into the
cold light of both moral and intellectual self-control,
Unamuno remains beyond, where the molten metal is
too near the fire of passion, and cannot cool down into
shape.

Unamuno is therefore not unlike Wordsworth in the
insufficiency of his sense of form. We have just seen
the essential cause of this insufficiency to lie in the
non-æsthetical attitude of his mind, and we have tried
to show one of the roots of such an attitude in the very
loftiness and earnestness of his purpose. Yet, there
are others, for living nature is many-rooted as it is
many-branched. It cannot be doubted that a certain
refractoriness to form is a typical feature of the
Basque character. The sense of form is closely in
sympathy with the feminine element in human nature.

and the Basque race is strongly masculine. The
predominance of the masculine element—strength
without grace—is as typical of Unamuno as it is of
Wordsworth. The literary gifts which might for the
sake of synthesis be symbolized in a smile are absent
in both. There is as little humour in the one as in
the other. Humour, however, sometimes occurs in
Unamuno, but only in his ill-humoured moments, and
then with a curious bite of its own which adds an
unconscious element to its comic effect. Grace only
visits them in moments of inspiration, and then it is
of a noble character, enhanced as it is by the ever-
present gift of strength. And as for the sense for
rhythm and music, both Unamuno and Wordsworth
seem to be limited to the most vigorous and masculine
gaits. This feature is particularly pronounced in
Unamuno, for while Wordsworth is painstaking, all-
observant, and too good a ' teacher ' to underestimate
the importance of pleasure in man's progress, Unamuno
knows no compromise. His aim is not to please but to
strike, and he deliberately seeks the naked, the forceful,
even the brutal word for truth. There is in him,
however, a cause of formlessness of which Wordsworth
is free—namely, an eagerness for sincerity and veracity
which brushes aside all preparation, ordering or
planning of ideas as suspect of ' dishing up ', intellectual
trickery, and juggling with spontaneous truths.

Such qualities—both the positive and the negative—
are apparent in his poetry. In it, the appeal of force
and sincerity is usually stronger than that of art. This
is particularly the case in his first volume (*Poesías*,
1907), in which a lofty inspiration, a noble attitude of
mind, a rich and racy vocabulary, a keen insight into
the spirit of places, and above all the overflowing
vitality of a strong man in the force of ripeness, contend against the still awkward gait of the Basque and

a certain rebelliousness of rhyme. The dough of the poetic language is here seen heavily pounded by a powerful hand, bent on reducing its angularities and on improving its plasticity. Nor do we need to wait for further works in order to enjoy the reward of such efforts, for it is attained in this very volume more than once, as for instance in *Muere en el mar el ave que voló del buque*, a beautiful poem in which emotion and thought are happily blended into exquisite form.

In his last poem, *El Cristo de Velázquez* (1920), Unamuno undertakes the task of giving a poetical rendering of his tragic sense of life, in the form of a meditation on the Christ of Velázquez, the beautiful and pathetic picture in the Prado. Why Velázquez's and not Christ himself ? The fact is that, though in his references to actual forms, Unamuno closely follows Velázquez's picture, the spiritual interpretation of it which he develops as the poem unfolds itself is wholly personal. It would be difficult to find two great Spaniards wider apart than Unamuno and Velázquez, for if Unamuno is the very incarnation of the masculine spirit of the North—all strength and substance— Valázquez is the image of the feminine spirit of the South—all grace and form. Velázquez is a limpid mirror, with a human depth, yet a mirror. That Unamuno has departed from the image of Christ which the great Sevillian reflected on his immortal canvas therefore was to be expected. But then Unamuno has, while speaking of Don Quixote, whom he has also freely and personally interpreted,[1] taken great care to point out that a work of art is, for each of us, all that we see in it. And, moreover, Unamuno has not so much departed from Velázquez's image of Christ as delved into its depths, expanded, enlarged it, or, if you prefer, seen in its limpid surface the immense

---

[1] *Vida de Don Quijote y Sancho, explicada y comentada*, por M. de Unamuno : Madrid, Fernando Fé, 1905.

figure of his own inner Christ. However free and
unorthodox in its wide scope of images and ideas, the
poem is in its form a regular meditation in the manner
approved by the Catholic Church, and it is therefore
meet that it should rise from a concrete, tangible
object as it is recommended to the faithful. To this
concrete character of its origin, the poem owes much
of its suggestiveness, as witness the following passage
quoted here, with a translation sadly unworthy of the
original, as being the clearest link between the poetical
meditation and the main thought that underlies all the
work and the life of Unamuno.

NUBE NEGRA

¿ O es que una nube negra de los cielos
ese negror le dió a tu cabellera
de nazareno, cual de mustio sauce
de una noche sin luna sobre el río ?
¿ Es la sombra del ala sin perfiles
del ángel de la nada negadora,
de Luzbel, que en su caída inacabable
— fondo no puede dar — su eterna cuita
clava en tu frente, en tu razón ?   ¿ Se vela
el claro Verbo en Ti con esa nube,
negra cual de Luzbel las negras alas,
mientras brilla el Amor, todo desnudo,
con tu desnudo pecho por cendal ?

BLACK CLOUD

Or was it then that a black cloud from heaven
Such blackness gave to your Nazarene's hair,
As of a languid willow o'er the river
Brooding in moonless night ?   Is it the shadow
Of the profileless wing of Luzbel, the Angel
Of denying nothingness, endlessly falling—
Bottom he ne'er can touch—whose grief eternal
He nails on to Thy forehead, to Thy reason ?
Is the clear Word in Thee with that cloud veiled
—A cloud as black as the black wings of Luzbel—
While Love shines naked within Thy naked breast ?

The poem, despite its length, easily maintains this lofty level throughout, and if he had written nothing else Unamuno would still remain as having given to Spanish letters the noblest and most sustained lyrical flight in the language. It abounds in passages of ample beauty, and often strikes a note of primitive strength in the true Old Testament style. It is most distinctively a poem in a major key, in a group with *Paradise Lost* and *The Excursion,* but in a tone half-way between the two ; and, as coming from the most Northern-minded and substantial poet that Spain ever had, wholly free from that tendency towards grandiloquence and Ciceronian drapery which blighted previous similar efforts in Spain. Its weakness lies in a certain monotony due to the interplay of Unamuno's two main limitations as an artist : the absolute surrender to one dominant thought and a certain deficiency of form bordering here on contempt. The plan is but a loose sequence of meditations on successive aspects of Christ as suggested by images or ascriptions of His Divine person, or even of parts of His human body : Lion, Bull, Lily, Sword, Crown, Head, Knees. Each meditation is treated in a period of blank verse, usually of a beautiful texture, the splendour of which is due less to actual images than to the inner vigour of ideas and the eagerness with which even the simplest facts are interpreted into significant symbols. Yet, sometimes, this blank verse becomes hard and stony under the stubborn hammering of a too insistent mind, and the device of ending each meditation with a line accented on its last syllable tends but to increase the monotony of the whole.

Blank verse is never the best medium for poets of a strong masculine inspiration, for it does not sufficiently correct their usual deficiency in form. Such poets are usually at their best when they bind themselves to the discipline of existing forms, and particu-

larly when they limit the movements of their muse to
the ' sonnet's scanty plot of ground '. Unamuno's best
poetry, as Wordsworth's, is in his sonnets. His
Rosario de Sonetos líricos, published in 1911, contains
some of the finest sonnets in the Spanish language.
There is variety in this volume—more at least than is
usual in Unamuno : from comments on events of
local politics (sonnet lii) which savour of the more
prosaic side of Wordsworth, to meditations on space
and time such as that sonnet xxxvii, so reminiscent of
Shelley's *Ozymandias of Egypt* ; from a suggestive
homily to a ' Don Juan of Ideas ' whose thirst for
knowledge is ' not love of truth, but intellectual lust·',
and whose ' thought is therefore sterile ' (sonnet cvii),
to an exquisitely rendered moonlight love scene
(sonnet civ). The author's main theme itself, which
of course occupies a prominent part in the series,
appears treated under many different lights and
in genuinely poetical moods which truly do justice to
the inherent wealth of poetical inspiration which it
contains. Many a sonnet might be quoted here, and
in particular that sombre and fateful poem *Nihil
Novum sub sole* (cxxiii), which defeats its own theme
by the striking originality of its inspiration.

So active, so positive is the inspiration of this poetry
that the question of outside influences does not even
arise. Unamuno is probably the Spanish contemporary poet whose manner owes least, if anything at
all, to modern developments of poetry such as those
which take their source in Baudelaire and Verlaine.
These over-sensitive and over-refined artists have no
doubt enriched the sensuous, the formal, the sentimental, even the intellectual aspects of verse with an
admirable variety of exquisite shades, lacking which
most poetry seems old-fashioned to the fastidious
palate of modern men. Unamuno is too genuine a
representative of the spiritual and masculine variety of

Spanish genius, ever impervious to French, and generally, to intellectual, influences, to be affected by the æsthetic excellence of this art. Yet, for all his disregard of the modern resources which it adds to the poetic craft, Unamuno loses none of his modernity. He is indeed more than modern. When, as he often does, he strikes the true poetic note, he is outside time. His appeal is not in complexity but in strength. He is not refined : he is final.

In the preface to his *Tres Novelas Ejemplares y un Prólogo* (1921) Unamuno says : ' . . . novelist—that is, poet . . . a novel—that is, a poem.' Thus, with characteristic decision, he sides with the lyrical conception of the novel. There is, of course, an infinite variety of types of novels. But they can probably all be reduced to two classes, i. e. the dramatic or objective, and the lyrical or subjective, according to the mood or inspiration which predominates in them. The present trend of the world points towards the dramatic or objective type. This type is more in tune with the detached and scientific character of the age. The novel is often nowadays considered as a document, a ' slice of life ', a piece of information, a literary photograph representing places and people which purse or time prevent us from seeing with our own eyes. It is obvious, given what we now know of him, that such a view of the novel cannot appeal to Unamuno. He is a utilitarian, but not of worldly utilities. His utilitarianism transcends our daily wants and seeks to provide for our eternal ones. He is, moreover, a mind whose workings turn in spiral form towards a central idea and therefore feels an instinctive antagonism to the dispersive habits of thought and sensation which such detailed observation of life usually entails. For at bottom the opposition between the lyrical and the dramatic novel may be reduced to that between the poet and the dramatist. Both the dramatist and the poet create in order to link up their soul and the world in one complete circle of experience, but this circle is travelled in opposite directions. The poet goes inward first, then out to nature full of his inner experience, and back home. The dramatist goes outwards first, then comes back to himself, his harvest of wisdom gathered in reality. It is the recognition of his own lyrical inward-looking nature which makes Unamuno pronounce the identity of the novel and the poem.

Whatever we may think of it as a general theory, there is little doubt that this opinion is in the main sound in so far as it refers to Unamuno's own work. His novels are created within. They are—and their author is the first to declare it so—novels which happen in the kingdom of the spirit. Outward points of reference in time and space are sparingly given—in fact, reduced to a bare minimum. In some of them, as for instance *Niebla* (1914), the name of the town in which the action takes place is not given, and such scanty references to the topography and general features as are supplied would equally apply to any other provincial town of Spain. Action, in the current sense of the word, is correspondingly simplified, since the material and local elements on which it usually exerts itself are schematized, and in their turn made, as it were, spiritual. Thus a street, a river of colour for some, for others a series of accurately described shops and dwellings, becomes in Unamuno (see *Niebla*) a loom where the passions and desires of men and women cross and recross each other and weave the cloth of daily life. Even the physical description of characters is reduced to a standard of the utmost simplicity. So that, in fine, Unamuno's novels, by eliminating all other material, appear, if the boldness of the metaphor be permitted, as the spiritual skeletons of novels, conflicts between souls.

Nor is this the last stage in his deepening and narrowing of the creative furrow. For these souls are, in their turn concentrated so that the whole of their vitality burns into one passion. If a somewhat fanciful comparison from another art may throw any light on this feature of his work, we might say that his characters are to those of Galdós, for instance, as counterpoint music to the complex modern symphony. Joaquín Monegro, the true hero of his *Abel Sánchez* (1917), is the personification of hatred. Raquel in *Dos Madres*[1] and Catalina in *El Marqués de Lumbría*[1] are two widely different but vigorous, almost barbarous, 'maternities'. Alejandro, the hero of his powerful *Nada menos que todo un Hombre*,[1] is masculine will, pure and unconquerable, save by death. Further still, in most if not all of his main characters, we can trace the dominant passion which is their whole being to a mere variety of the one and only passion which obsesses Unamuno himself, the hunger for life, a full life, here and after. Here is, for instance, *Abel Sánchez*, a sombre study of hatred, a modern paraphrase of the story of Cain. Joaquín Monegro, the Cain of the novel, has been reading Byron's poem, and writes in his diary : ' When I read how Lucifer declared to Cain that he, Cain, was immortal, is when I began in terror to wonder whether I also was immortal and whether in me would be also immortal my hatred. " Have I a soul ? " I said to myself then. " Is this my hatred soul ? " And I came to think that it could not be otherwise, that such a hatred cannot be a function of the body. . . . A corruptible organism could not hate as I hated.'[2]

---

[1] These three novels appeared together as *Tres Novelas y un Prólogo* : Calpe, Madrid, 1921.

[2] Cuando leí cómo Luzbel le declaraba a Caín cómo era este, Caín, inmortal, es cuando empecé con terror a pensar, si yo también seré inmortal y si será inmortal en mí mi odio. ' ¿ Tendré alma ? '—me

Thus Joaquín Monegro, like every other main character in his work, appears preoccupied by the same central preoccupation of Unamuno. In one word, all Unamuno's characters are but incarnations of himself. But that is what we expected to find in a lyrical novelist.

There are critics who conclude from this observation that these characters do not exist, that they are mere arguments on legs, personified ideas. Here and there, in Unamuno's novels, there are passages which lend some colour of plausibility to this view. Yet, it is in my opinion mistaken. Unamuno's characters may be schematized, stripped of their complexities, reduced to the mainspring of their nature ; they may, moreover, reveal mainsprings made of the same steel. But that they are alive no one could deny who has a sense for life. The very restraint in the use of physical details which Unamuno has made a feature of his creative work may have led his critics to forget the intensity of those—admirably chosen—which are given. It is significant that the eyes play an important part in his description of characters and in his narrative too. His sense of the interpenetration of body and soul is so deep that he does not for one moment let us forget how bodily his ' souls ' are, and how pregnant with spiritual significance is every one of their words and gestures. No. These characters are not arguments on legs. They truly are men and women of ' flesh and bones ', human, terribly human.

In thus emphasizing a particular feature in their nature, Unamuno imparts to his creations a certain deformity which savours of romantic days. Yet Unamuno is not a romanticist, mainly because Roman-

dije entonces—' ¿ Será este mi odio alma ? ' y llegué a pensar que no podía ser de otro modo, que no puede ser función de un cuerpo un odio así. . . . Un organismo corruptible no podía odiar como yo odiaba (*Abel Sánchez*, p. 85).

ticism was an æsthetic attitude, and his attitude is seldom purely æsthetic. For all their show of passion true Romanticists seldom gave their real selves to their art. They created a stage double of their own selves for public exhibitions. They sought the picturesque. Their form was lyrical, but their substance was dramatic. Unamuno, on the contrary, even though he often seeks expression in dramatic form, is essentially lyrical. And if he is always intense, he never is exuberant. He follows the Spanish tradition for restraint—for there is one, along with its opposite tradition for grandiloquence—and, true to the spirit of it, he seeks the maximum of effect through the minimum of means. Then he never shouts. Here is an example of his quiet method, the rhythmical beauty of which is unfortunately almost untranslatable :

' Y así pasaron días de llanto y de negrura hasta que las lágrimas fueron yéndose hacia adentro y la casa fué derritiendo los negrores ' (*Niebla*). (And thus, days of weeping and mourning went by, till the tears began to flow inward and the blackness to melt in the home.)

Miguel de Unamuno is to-day the greatest literary figure of Spain. Baroja may surpass him in variety of external experience, Azorín in delicate art, Ortega y Gasset in philosophical subtlety, Ayala in intellectual elegance, Valle Inclán in rhythmical grace. Even in vitality he may have to yield the first place to that overwhelming athlete of literature, Blasco Ibáñez. But Unamuno is head and shoulders above them all in the highness of his purpose and in the earnestness and loyalty with which, Quixote-like, he has served all through his life his unattainable Dulcinea. Then there is another and most important reason which explains his position as first, *princeps*, of Spanish letters, and it is that Unamuno, by the cross which he has chosen to bear, incarnates the spirit of modern Spain. His eternal conflict between faith and reason, between life and thought, between spirit and intellect, between heaven and civilization, is the conflict of Spain herself. A border country, like Russia, in which East and West mix their spiritual waters, Spain wavers between two life-philosophies and cannot rest. In Russia, this conflict emerges in literature during the nineteenth century, when Dostoievsky and Tolstoy stand for the East while Turgeniev becomes the West's advocate. In Spain, a country less articulate, and moreover, a country in which the blending of East and West is more intimate, for both found a common solvent in centuries of Latin civilization, the conflict is less clear, less on the surface. To-day Ortega y Gasset is our Turgeniev—not without mixture. Unamuno is our Dostoievsky, but painfully aware of the strength of the other side within him, and full of misgivings. Nor is it sure that when we speak of East in this connexion we really mean East. There is a third country in Europe in which the ' Eastern ' view is as forcibly put and as deeply understood as the ' Western ', a third border country—England. England, particularly in those of her racial elements conventionally named Celtic, is closely in sympathy with the ' East '. Ireland is almost purely ' Eastern ' in this respect. That is perhaps why Unamuno feels so strong an attraction for the English language and its literature, and why, even to this day, he follows so closely the movements of English thought. For his own life-work, as a human being astride two enemy ideals, draws him instinctively towards minds equally placed in opposition, yet a co-operating opposition, to progress. Thus Unamuno, whose literary qualities and defects make him a genuine representative of the more masculine variety of the Spanish genius, becomes in his spiritual life the true living symbol of his country and his time. And that he is great enough to bear this incarnation is a sufficient measure of his greatness.

PIO BAROJA

IN one of his latest books—*Youth, Self-worship* [1]—
Don Pio Baroja describes himself as an Arch-European.
This ' Arch ' should suffice to arouse the suspicions of
the least watchful of his readers. Why paint a natural
lily ? The emphasizing prefix bears all the aspect of
an over-anxious grip on the title lest it be snatched
away from the not too sure holder of it. In order to
establish his claims to this proud title, Baroja defines
Europe in a somewhat arbitrary fashion, limiting it to
the lands that stretch between the Pyrenees and the
Alps. And as he—so he informs us—is seven-eighths
Basque and one-eighth Lombard, no purer Arch-
European could of course be found in *that* Europe
than the author of some of the most striking and
widely read of modern Spanish novels.

Yet, after all, there are better definitions of Europe,
both geographical and psychological, than that which
would limit it to several provinces of Southern France,
Northern Italy, and Northern Spain. As Baroja
himself well knows [2], what we nowadays mean by
Europe is above all a conscious (and even self-conscious) mind, capable of a continuous and ordered
effort towards the understanding of the Universe.
Now, it takes very little knowledge of the Basque
race to realize that neither continuity, nor order, nor
the predominance of the conscious are amongst its
specific features. Baroja has therefore to chose between
his ' Arch-European ' claim and his Basque blood.
As making up his mind is not his forte, nature decides
for him. Baroja is a Basque.

[1] *Juventud, Egolatría* (1917).
[2] Cf. *Divagaciones sobre la cultura*.

The Spanish Basque country is a region in which hard, primitive formations predominate. It is angular and broken, intersected by narrow, deep valleys, running between hills crowned here and there by an isolated *caserío*. The landscape leaves on the mind an impression of narrowness and isolation. Angularity, narrowness, earnestness, and a strong individualistic sense, appear also in the character of the Basque people. The combination of all these tendencies results in a typically Basque feature : loyalty. The loyalty of the Basque is an historical byword. But there are many kinds of loyalty. That of the Basque seems due to the national proclivity towards what might be described as mental or moral absolutism, i. e. the recognition of the indisputable supremacy of one value over all others. Needless to say, this is a most un-European feature. ' Culture ', i.e. the due appreciation of the Universe, requires a harmonious mind, capable of reflecting in its own complexity the complexities of nature. But the Basque is not endowed with such a gift. He naturally tends towards a mono-theistic or absolutist turn of mind, and surrenders unreservedly to the idea which overlords him. With the great majority of the Basque people this High Idea is no other than that Catholic God into whose hands the great Basque captain, Loyola, surrendered his life. Any one of the great Basques of the day, Unamuno, Baroja, Maeztu, would have been a monk in Loyola's time. But Baroja was born too late, and he finds himself out of tune with his time. Life gave him birth in the Century of Lights, and so, with the same singlemindedness, the same courage, and the same uncompromising fierceness with which Loyola fought for Christ in the sixteenth century, Pio Baroja, born in the nineteenth century, battles for Truth.

The arms of the Knight of Christ could be either prayer or the sword. The arm of the Knight of

Truth is his pen. And the first care of Pio Baroja
is to purify his pen from all worldly ambitions. What
more worldly than Rhetoric ? Baroja fears Rhetoric
almost as much as Loyola the Devil. And he takes
of the one no less strict a view than Loyola did of the
other. He never condescends to please. Not only
does he banish from his style all adventitious ornament,
but he even refrains from yielding to the slightest of
those waverings with which the natural instinct for
rhythm and expression tends to animate the curve of
form. Not content thus to deprive his works of both
painted and natural flowers, he seems almost deliberately to cultivate a graceless delivery, even to the
point of ungrammatical slovenliness. He has been
accused by unkind, though superficial, critics of
ignorance of Spanish. The reasons which explain his
careless and formless style are more numerous and
deeper. They must be sought in his race, his character,
and his absolute, nay, his fanatical devotion to Truth.
As a true Basque, Baroja has a peasant nature and
finds himself most at home in simple surroundings.
He has expressed the attractiveness of refined society
in words full of that almost naïve sincerity which is
perhaps his main literary asset.

An after-dinner table talk, a little animated, is something
which seduces and attracts. A dining-room in a private
house, with luxury ; eight or ten guests, three or four
pretty women, some of them foreign ; as many men, none
of whom should be an aristocrat—for aristocrats are as a rule
very unentertaining—nor an artist—for they are of the same
caste as the aristocrats ; to be sitting next to some banker or
Jew with an aquiline profile, and to talk about life, politics ;
to be a little courtly with the ladies ; to let each have his
opportunity to shine ; that is no doubt a very agreeable
thing.[1]

[1] Una sobremesa un poco animada es algo que seduce y atrae. Un
comedor de una casa particular, lujoso ; ocho o diez convidados, tres
o cuatro mujeres bonitas, alguna de ellas extranjera ; otros tantos

This is truly peasant-like in its awkward simplicity.
No clearer document is needed to show that, for
Baroja, refinement is on a higher plane than nature,
difficult to attain, still more to keep. And thus the
carelessness and primitiveness of his style appear at
first as the easiest path for a nature poorly gifted with
the sense of refinement. This racial characteristic
takes in Baroja a certain boorish aspect which is
peculiar to his own individual nature. Baroja is a
solitary man, and, like most solitary men, he tends to
divide the world into two parts : himself, and the rest.
Hence an exaggerated, if perhaps unconscious, sense
of the importance of his ways and a tendency to strike
the world by saying unusually hard things in an unusually
hard way. Since the general trend of the Southern
mind, which tends to overrule Spanish literature, is
towards splendour of form, Baroja will be dry. And
since most of us are weak enough to enjoy the implicit
flattery which we detect in an author's efforts to
please, Baroja will be terribly independent and refuse
to smile. Thus, his style is as uncompromising as his
matter, and words and sentences are served raw, with
a ' take it or leave it ' gesture full of an independence
bordering on ill temper which is, on the whole, amusing
and does no harm to his books. Nor is it possible to
pass by this feature of Baroja's work without connecting
his contempt for form with that monkish contempt for
the world which is so deeply ingrained in the Basque
mind. Thus Baroja's style is but the twentieth-
century manifestation of a tendency which, in the

hombres, que ninguno sea aristócrata — porque los aristócratas son
muy poco amenos en general — ni sea tampoco artista — porque son
de la misma casta de los aristócratas ; tener de vecino a algun banquero
o a algun judío de perfil aguileño, y hablar de la vida, de la política,
estar un poco galante con las señoras, dejar que cada uno tenga un
momento de lucimiento, es, sin duda alguna, cosa muy agradable
(*Juventud, Egolatría,* p. 119).

sixteenth century, would have made him wear a hair shirt and eat stale bread and spinach boiled in water without salt.

Were there none but negative features in his style no one would read him. Yet Baroja is widely read and daily gains ground. This, in so far as style is concerned, is due to the fact that in renouncing most of the attractive methods of the literary art, he has gained a freer scope for the intensity and power of his vision. The result is a writing which for directness and simplicity has no rival in Spain. Baroja merely states. There are whole pages in his novels which are but a succession of facts, noted in short sentences which sound like the steady fall of packets that are being unloaded in a factory. Not the slightest attempt at explaining them, relating them, exploiting them for emotional, critical, or historical purposes within the novel. Things seen and done pass unconnectedly before the eyes of the reader and the tone of the narrator never wavers, never warms up. There is no doubt in all this a scruple for truthfulness. Baroja, the Knight of Truth, fears lest any development of the fact for the sake of æsthetical construction might ultimately destroy the freshness of the first impression. But it must be owned that in this restraint from all further manipulation of the vital fact, there is also a Basque incapacity for following up the promptings of the soul touched by reality, and for grouping them into a system, whether æsthetical or philosophical. Baroja instinctively feels that the Basque soul is at its highest when reacting on an impact from the world. He therefore gives us a quick succession of first impressions and does not allow himself to dwell on any point of reality one second longer than the indispensable minimum to see, feel, and note down. He himself has commented on this incapacity for literary development in a passage typical both for its penetration of the bare fact and for the critical inability of his mind to receive and express it.

When my critical sense heightens I often think : if I had now to write those books, now that I see their defects, I would not write them. And yet, I go on writing new ones with the same old faults. Shall I ever attain that spiritual ripeness in which the intensity of the impression endures, and yet one can render the expression more perfect ? I believe not. Probably, when I arrive at wanting to subtilize (*alambicar*) my expression I shall have nothing to say and I shall keep silent.[1]

The result is at first a little disconcerting. Yet, there is perhaps in this manner of writing a greater capacity for effect than hurried readers—especially if endowed with an intellectual tradition—would be ready to grant. Baroja's style after all is to the traditional style of novel-writing what that of contemporary musicians is to classical music. Nowadays, the classical construction by means of themes developed and interwoven in continuous fashion, has yielded to a more direct expression by means of musical phrases rising when necessary and merging back into the harmonic mass as soon as their message has been delivered. So Baroja, probably without having ever thought of this analogy with modern music, and led purely by the group of causes which we have tried to analyse, came to write his novels in a disconnected succession of short episodes, having no particular rhythm or shape, beginning just anyhow and ending just any way, having no other relations than those between the characters which run through them, and no other unity than a vague continuity in

---

[1] Cuando se me exacerba el sentido crítico suelo pensar : Si ahora tuviera que hacer estos libros, ahora que veo sus defectos, no los haría. Sin embargo, sigo haciendo otros con las mismas faltas antiguas. ¿ Llegaré alguna vez a esa madurez espiritual en que perdura la intensidad de las sensaciones y se puede perfeccionar la expresión ? Creo que nó. Probablemente, cuando llegue a querer alambicar la expresión, no tendré nada que decir y callaré (*Juventud, Egolatría*, p. 57).

time and the mood of the whole novel which they build
up ultimately by their cumulative effect.

In either case, the guiding impulse is one towards
truth. With the musicians, mostly French, who led
the modern evolution of their art, we may assume this
impulse towards truth to emanate from that same
intellectual tendency to a close-fitting correspondence
between thought and reality which is the most
prominent feature of French genius, and constitutes
as it were the axial line of European progress. But
we could by no stretch of imagination attribute to an
equal cause the truth-seeking eagerness of Baroja,
and thus, we must explain it in a way more in harmony
with the literary traditions of his race and with the
features of his own character. Now, it is obvious that
Baroja's realism has its roots in the realism which is
typical of Spanish literature throughout its history.
There is a sense in which the author of such novels
as that vivid trilogy of picaresque life which bears the
name of ' La Lucha por la Vida ' [1] may be said to
be the direct descendant of the authors of *Lazarillo
de Tormes* and *Guzmán de Alfarache*. Realism is
generally the healthy reaction of a community against
its own tendency to hide away its more unpleasant
aspects. It is therefore but natural that eagerness for
truth in a novelist should manifest itself in the emphasizing of the sordid side of reality. The picaresque novels
and Baroja have this feature in common. Baroja seems
to prefer for his subjects the evils which seethe in an
atmosphere of destitution. No other Spanish author
has dwelt more frequently and insistently on the
peculiar aspect which human nature takes under the
grey twilight ever hovering over the borders of hunger.
Hunger and poverty were also familiar subjects with
the picaresque authors, but how differently treated !
For, though picaresque in many of his subjects,

[1] The three novels are *La Busca*, *Mala Hierba*, and *Aurora Roja*.

Baroja can hardly be described as such if the mood be considered in which he approaches them. The picaresque authors were wholly indifferent to the ethical aspects of the life they depicted. True, they often overburdened their narrative with sermons suggesting that their only concern in writing of evil things was to show how abhorrent vice really is ; but it is doubtful whether these sermons were ever taken at their face value even by the inquisition officials to whose wary eyes they were really directed, and the sermon once over, the story went on gaily and remorselessly. Baroja, on the other hand, is deeply concerned with the ethical monstrosity of the horrors which he illustrates. Nor is his concern due to any hard and fast theory of conduct. On ethics his ideas seem to be as fluid, nay, as confused, as in all other realms of human thought. What troubles him is not sin but suffering. It is the sight of humanity dishonoured by disease, divided by crime and brute authority, left to her weakness, tricked by nature, exposed to the animal shame of hunger.

This aspect of the ugly side of nature seems to haunt Baroja. He sees it with an acuity in which the pitiless genius for observation of the Spanish race is mingled with the professional training of the doctor of medicine. In him, the medical man is ever in company with the novelist. Few men start life with the settled intention of becoming artists, and therefore the number of artists who are trained for a profession is relatively high. The influence of professional training over artists is one of those by-questions of criticism which would repay study. There is little doubt that doctors are handicapped in their artistic development by a scientific training which plunges them so deep in the most material recesses of human nature. The sciences of the body which constitute the ground of all medical education study the physical terminals of human nature, just as the sciences of the spirit—theology, metaphysics, poetry—deal with its spiritual terminals. It is small wonder that doctors should evince a tendency to interpret everything human in terms of bodily phenomena, and, when literary men, that they should use their pen as a dissecting knife. One thing doctors cannot do, that is obtain a living synthesis. Thus, a purely professional handicap is added to that natural incapacity for organic work which we have observed in Baroja, while the habit of looking at human miseries with the cool eye of the doctor adds a touch of the hospital clinic to his realism.

This is not, however, a reflection on Baroja's sensibility. Far from being an insensitive man, he is rather a repressed sentimentalist, who refuses to show his feeling, partly from pride, partly from timidity, partly from a self-conscious fear of the ridicule attached to sentiment in a country in which fire is more prized than water. But though not expressed nor even admitted, feeling is there as it were in an undercurrent, or rather in a parallel current. Baroja tells things plainly and coldly, but in a tone which unmistakably comments : ' Now, if you don't think that horrible you are a brute.' Like all men whose feelings are restrained by the fear of losing their liberty in reciprocity—a usual enough situation with ultra-individualists—Baroja bestows the best of his tenderness on such creatures as cannot reciprocate in terms of equality. Hence his love of animals and children. Throughout his work, harm done to children or animals is sharply brought into relief in all its naked repulsiveness with an intensity due to true feeling. But this feature of Baroja's sensibility is linked up with his general attitude towards the world and its evil.

There is in Baroja's latent protest against the sufferings of children and animals a touch of irritation at the irrationality of a world in which such things can happen. It is a mere heightening of his general attitude to all evil, due partly to a sentimental cause—his special solicitude for the victims—partly also to a logical cause—that, in the case of defenceless and innocent victims, the monstrosity and uncalled-for character of evil is most repellent. Here, therefore, we find the earnestness of the Basque mind. In his critical attitude towards the world Baroja is closely akin to Dostoievsky, who seems to have exerted a strong if limited influence over him. This earnestness of his outlook, and the uncompromising way in which he keeps to his level and refuses to waste time on minor matters, constitute the positive element of his art. We go to Baroja knowing that his novels deal with acts and motives that matter. We go to him knowing that, right or wrong, he is sincere, and that no tradition, no prejudice, no social respect will prevail upon his sense of truth.

And yet, having read him with more respect than real pleasure, we come to the conclusion that there is something unsatisfactory about his work. Our first objection may be summed up in one word : disorder. This style, the directness of which we duly value, strikes us as more than merely careless. It is unequal. Here and there tense and fitting closely to the matter, it becomes now and then loose and distracted, vague and uncontrolled by thought. At moments we guess the meaning by the general direction of thought as we guess the aim of a bad hitter by the direction of his eyes. But the words are wide of the mark. Improvisation, a Spanish habit which explains much that is bad and even a little of the good in Spanish literature, is frequently the cause of these lapses of Baroja's style. More often than not his books flow from him ' al correr de la pluma ', as the saying goes. But there is in the unevenness of his style something more than mere carelessness and improvisation. It

is unequal not only in that it evinces differences of
level within the same quality, but in that it results
from a mixture of qualities. His general tendency is
towards bareness and simplicity. Often, both in his
critical works and in the explanatory pages on style
and composition which he is wont to insert in the
midst of his narratives, he pours contempt on
' rhetoric ', by which he means, amongst other
really contemptible things, all attempts at raising
expression above a mere statement of fact. But he
nevertheless allows himself full freedom to forget
his theories and so breaks out unexpectedly into such
' rhetorical ' pranks as elaborate descriptions of landscape and even pseudo-lyrical flights which he naïvely
recommends to the attention of the reader by the
simple device of adding a few dots to the paragraph. . . .
And thus the mere examination of his style brings us
to the conclusion that it is the expression of a mind
which has little natural clearness and little also of that
acquired clearness which is at bottom what we understand by ' culture '.

Baroja usually speaks of culture in terms of almost
awestruck respect which come as a surprise from the
pen of so ill-tempered an iconoclast. ' I look upon
Ortega y Gasset as the wayfarer who has travelled into
the lands of culture. It is a higher step which is
difficult to attain and still more difficult to establish
oneself on.' [1] This sentence may be put alongside
of the one already quoted, in which he expresses his
pleasure in refined society. Needless to say, Baroja
is far from being an ignorant man. Not only does he
possess the professional knowledge of a doctor of

---

[1] Ortega y Gasset es para mí el viajero que ha hecho el viaje por
las tierras de la cultura. Es un escalón más alto al que es difícil llegar
y más difícil aun afianzarse en él (*Juventud, Egolatría*, p. 244). The
ungrammatical form of the translation is a deliberate imitation of the
original.

medicine, but he has read widely, scientific as well
as philosophic and literary books, both old and new.
Yet, despite all this reading, he can hardly be described
as a cultured man. There is something in his nature
which seems to be as rebellious to culture as it is to
refinement. It is probably that same incapacity for
following up first inspirations, impressions, thoughts,
and weaving them into a complex unity.

A curious feature of his character renders relatively
easy the search for lacunæ in his powers. There is
a pride in him which leads him to minimize or ridicule,
or both, whatever force he feels he does not possess.
And in his curious antagonism towards France we may
perhaps find the root of his refractoriness to culture.
France is one of the favourite objects of his scorn.
That he attacks her on the weak spots of her armour
merely shows that he is a skilful enemy. We are not,
however, concerned here with the strategy of his attack,
but with the psychological roots of his enmity. And
these must be found in the contrast between the spirit
of France and that of Baroja. Imagine this Basque
primitive mind, with all the finesse, all the shrewd
penetration into the character of the peasant, but also
with all the peasant's rusticity, by the side of Racine.
France means not only the spirit of balance, the sense
of measure and proportions, that is, ultimately, the
sense of form, but further, all the qualities which
result from the application to life of the sense of form
and the spirit of balance. Life in France is not the
raw passional stuff which Baroja likes to observe, but
that stuff shaped and fashioned by a trained intellect,
or, in a word, refinement. That paragraph of Baroja's
on after-dinner talk is but a rough sketch, a kind of
cave-picture, of the French *salon*. In France, by the
action of centuries of refinement, the world is naturally
seen in an intellectual order which gives a majesty and
a harmony to what otherwise would be a chaos as

formless, if as lively, as one of Baroja's novels. This capacity for intellectual vision has been denied Baroja, and the lack of it is apparent not only in the loose texture of his style and in his utter lack of all sense of composition, but also in a certain feeling of helplessness which is never absent from the intellect that has not found its bearings as from the heart that has not found its faith.

For, gallant as are his efforts to impress his readers with the courage of a modern *esprit fort* who dares proclaim his atheism without lifting his arm lest Heaven should fall on his head, Baroja is nevertheless a child, and we can hear his voice tremble whenever he shouts towards the void. His hatred for priests and all kinds of religion can only be compared superficially with that shallow rationalism which the indiscriminate spread of so-called education tends to foster in Spain as elsewhere. It is a hatred with a personal touch in it, a hatred which can be best explained by Unamuno's penetrating remark that most rationalists, ' possessed by the rage of being unable to believe, fall into the irritation of an *odium antitheologicum* '.[1] Now, this irritation itself belongs to the religious, not to the ' cultural ' or scientific order, which of itself is dispassionate and calm. Hence an amusing discord within Baroja's attitude towards religion and its ministers. For while he dismisses the one and the other as vestiges of error and superstition, he does so in a manner which strangely resembles that which it means to disown. But of these contradictions between manner and substance, between thought and the vital texture of thought, the Basque race in general and Baroja in particular, present abundant examples.

Deprived of a religious explanation of the world,

---

[1] *El Sentimiento Trágico de la Vida*, p. 97.

Baroja turns to science. He is too intelligent to
expect from science an answer to the riddle of the
world, but he comes to science because it is made of
the very stuff of truth and also because he is proud
and feels that in science man is grown up and looks
straight in front of him, not upwards, as in religion.
There is a book of his—*Paradox, King*—in which he
has tried to express in a humorous form this belief in
science as the organizing element of the world.
Silvestre Paradox, a hero borrowed from one of his
earlier novels, is but a transfiguration of Pio Baroja
himself. It is, therefore, worth while observing the
name chosen by Baroja for his literary double:
boorishness is expressed in the Christian name—
Silvestre; self-imagined originality in face of a gaping
world, in the name—Paradox. Silvestre Paradox,
however, deserves his Christian name better than his
patronymic, for his ideas could hardly sound paradoxical outside the *Casino Tradicionalista* of Itzea,
the village in which Baroja himself, as a terrible
atheist, is known by the name of ' The Bad Man '.
He is a simple, kindly, boorish, and solitary man, fond
of animals and children, who hates all cant and
hypocrisy and believes that it is easier to conquer
negroes by showing them the advantages of civilization than by shooting them down under martial law.
There is an undercurrent of political criticism, though
discreet, irrelevant, in this tale of an expedition to
Africa in the course of which a group of Spanish,
French, and English adventurers fall into the hands of
a cannibal tribe and pass from the chief's larder to
high positions of power and authority through sheer
superiority of mind and will. This idea of reason as
the guiding light of the world of men is expanded by
Baroja to embrace all nature, and results in a picture
in which every stone, tree, animal, star, man, voices
his own point of view. Yet here, in his scientific

mood, no less than in his creative capacity, Baroja fails to unite, to make a whole out of his cacophony of separate voices. As a thinker no less than as an artist he remains in the first stage of perception, a recorder of disconnected facts.

On the intellectual side, this feature is due to a lack of what the French call *esprit de suite*. On the creative side, it results from that all-important deficiency in Baroja's character as an artist : his utter lack of lyrical power. Here again, were we not made aware of it on every page by the loveless tone of his writings, Baroja would of himself draw our attention to the weak spot by his constant scornful remarks on poetry :

> It was . . . the hour in which the poet thinks on immortality, rhyming *wind* with *unkind* and *love* with *dove*.[1]

Such sentences reveal in Baroja an underworld of antipoetical feeling similar to his feelings against religion and against France—three revelations respectively of his lack of poetry, of religion, and of refinement. No Spaniard ever lived farther away from the hearth whereon the fire which gives warmth and glow to all the arts burns in generous flames of love—for love is after all the spirit of poetry and poetry the spirit of all art. Baroja is an excellent illustration of this truth, so often forgotten in criticism, that sensitiveness is not necessarily love. He is genuinely sensitive, not merely æsthetically, but humanly and ethically so. He is, indeed, far more sensitive as a man than as an artist. Yet, he is loveless. His sensitiveness is purely receptive and never results in an outgoing flow of feeling. It adds to his burden of pain—a pain in which the physical and the mental elements predominate over the emotional ; but it never brings him any pleasure. His reaction to nature's sights and

[1] Era . . . la hora en que el poeta piensa en la inmortalidad, rimando *hijos* con *prolijos* y *amor* con *dolor* (*La Busca*, p. 10).

doings, particularly to those of human nature, is
we feel, a kind of shrinking, as of a nerve that is being
irritated by an experimenter ; never of that expanding
quality which is the privilege of great, all-embracing
hearts. He carries into his views of love that unfortunate absorption by the physical which is the hall-
mark of his medical· studies and tends to degrade all
affection to the level of disease or of vice. His attitude
towards women is free and masterful enough when he
deals with the lowest types of feminine degradation.
But when he attempts to rise higher in the spiritual
scale he is awkward, distant, and scornful, with an
undercurrent of repressed irritation always ready to
burst out into the open. True to his physiological
interpretation of man-and-woman love, he seems to
incline towards that type of masculine, headstrong
woman with which Mr. Bernard Shaw has peopled
the contemporary English stage and Tirso before him
the stage of the Spanish Golden Century. It is a
type which only hopeless sentimentalists can overlook
in life, and with which only hopeless sentimentalists
can be fascinated to the point of overlooking all others.
For it requires all the sentimentalist's secret hatred
of love—living love, with its wars and its peaces, its
prides and its humilities—to reduce all love to the
level of a Darwinian law. It is this absence of all
sense of love, whether human or divine, which dries
up the springs of poetry in Baroja. Feeling is there
and moves darkly in the recesses of his being. But he
will not let go. He is a grown-up man, an Arch-European, believing in reason and no sentiment. And as
he thinks more of what he is than of what he would
fain feel if only he dared, poetry in him is stillborn.

A curious trilogy of paradoxes, this author of
trilogies, this creator of Silvestre Paradox. He is
a sentimentalist without love ; an ' Arch-European '
without culture ; a rationalist with a true religious

hatred of priests. He gave himself as his high aim
a fearless devotion to Truth. Yet, lacking in refinement, in philosophical *esprit de suite*, and in poetical
feeling, which are the social, the mental, and the
æsthetic avenues towards a synthetic view of life,
our uncompromising Knight of Truth is denied the
full sight of his Lady's face, and he must remain
content to catch whatever glimpses of her he can espy
in the by-streets of the world.

Baroja is eminently a *modern* novelist. There was
a time when men delighted in works of art and sought
in them either the exhilaration of life re-felt and
recreated by the power of an emotional spirit or the
quiet enjoyment of a harmonious grouping of natural
elements selected by a serenely creative mind. Nowadays, art ministers to wholly different wants. We
are neither Dyonisian nor Apollinian. We are devotees
of Minerva. We do not want to feel, we do not want
to enjoy. We want to know. We suspect the artist
because we feel, and rightly, that he may twist reality
to his own ends. Yet we are aware that there is such
a thing as æsthetic knowledge, and even that it is
probably the most satisfactory of all the ways of
knowing. Our ideal approach to reality through our
æsthetic sense is therefore by means of a sensitive
author lacking constructional power and all sense of
development. Such an author is like a physical
instrument which we plunge into the depths of human
nature, knowing that it will report true. Baroja
answers almost perfectly to these requirements. His
love of truth thus appears as the functional instinct
of a human instrument for measuring life by means of
a living sensibility. Baroja is, in fine, a living *biometer*.
Such a view of his utility and function as an author
ought to commend itself to his love of science. It is
at any rate truly Arch-European.

RAMÓN MARÍA DEL VALLE INCLÁN

THERE is to the north-west of the Spanish Peninsula a land in which the Pyrenean Range, having prevailed over the ocean for some hundreds of miles from the point where it leaves the French mainland at Fuenterrabía, is at last unable to resist the onslaught of the water and breaks into shreds. In this land, earth and sea are intimately intertwined, forming sea-lochs which the natives characteristically name by feminizing the Spanish for *river*: they are the quiet, poetical *rías* of Galicia. Here, the hard, rocky spirit of northern Spain is softened down by the winds which blow from the sea, warmed by the western stream and laden with a moisture which clothes hills and valleys with a rich mantle of verdure. The knotty oak and the leafy chestnut-tree people the flanks and the heights of the undulating hills, while long lines of trembling birches accompany ever abundant and murmuring rivers. The valleys are wide, the hills not too imposing, and the light is filtered by the delicate veils which the fairies of the water weave in the air—now an invisible moisture, now a grey mist, now woolly fogs, now a silk-threaded rain which hangs silently. Neither too narrow, as in the Basque mountains, nor too wide as in the Castilian plains, the landscape has just the spaciousness and the limitations required for companionship and common life. It is alive but peaceful, quiet but murmuring with the murmurs of water, beast, and man and the rustling waverings of the foliage.

The name of this land—Galicia—is philologically

connected with all those names—Portugal, Gaul, Gallic, Gaelic, Wales, Wallon—which suggest a more or less vague relationship of race or language or both, between several peoples of Western Europe. It is, therefore, a favourite country for the vagaries of the Celtomaniac, and, to believers in the myth of the Blonde Beast, it even offers the alluring fact of a distant domination by the Germanic tribe of the Suevi, who seem to have left a trace of their passage in the occasional occurrence of red-haired and blue-eyed types of great physical beauty. However that may be, there is little doubt that the Gallegan and the Castilian types differ profoundly, both in language and in character. The Gallegan language may be shortly described as Portuguese free from the nasal developments which true Portuguese evolved under French influence. Gallegan is thus softer and more melodious than Castilian, and as superior to Castilian in lyrical quality as inferior to it in dramatic power. In so far as literature is concerned, the same comparison may be established between Gallegan and Castilian character. It is now generally admitted that Castilian poetry was naturally born epic and dramatic and that it received its lyrical strain from Galicia, so much so that Castilian poets, of whatever part of Castile, sang their first lyrical attempts in Gallegan, even when they used Castilian for the more utilitarian aims of narrating and moralizing.

The admirable efflorescence of the Gallegan muse which took place in the thirteenth and fourteenth centuries has been sometimes explained as being due to the influence of Provençal poetry, which would have been conveyed as far as Galicia along that most frequented of mediaeval thoroughfares, the pilgrim-road to St. James of Compostela. The hypothesis is both insufficient and unnecessary, for, while it does not explain why Provençal influence should not have raised similar fruits of lyrical poetry in those parts of the long trail of pilgrim-road remaining outside Galicia, it overlooks the fact that in its most truly felt and moving, as well as in its most original, varieties, Gallegan lyrical poetry was popular, that is, born in the layers least likely to be reached by an art expressed in a foreign language. There is, moreover, a striking difference in spirit between the two kinds of poetry, for, while form in the art of Provence is drawn out according to intellectual devices, form in Gallegan poetry is inspired by a musical feeling which is so closely in harmony with the character of the country that its main features remain to this day as typically its own. The natural conclusion is, therefore, that this poetry, however much it may have been stimulated by foreign influences, owes its origin to tendencies inherent in the race and land in which it flourished.

In its sense of melody, in its quaint grace, in its gift of emotion, the poetry of Galicia is distinctly un-Castilian. Two remarks made on its mediaeval forms remain true to this day. It is a poetry concerned with love almost to the exclusion of any other theme, and it is generally conceived from the point of view of women, often indeed created by women. Thus, it is three times feminine : in its point of view (if not in its actual origin) ; in the predominance of the subject of love ; and in its tenderness. We may add another feminine feature, a sense of form which is not external and intellectual, but internal and musical, and directly due to emotion.

In the nineteenth century Galicia has shown the persistence of all these features of her poetry by giving to Spanish letters a poetess of genius, Rosalía Castro, whose poems are the richest in genuine emotion and the most original in melody and form which Spanish poetry has produced in modern times, before the advent of the contemporary school with the Spanish-American

Rubén Darío. The Gallegan spirit is to-day admirably though less faithfully represented in Spanish letters by a poet and novelist of great talent, imagination, and artistic ability : Don Ramón María del Valle Inclán.

A good name is as necessary to a poet as a good frame to a picture. A mere façade! Maybe. Yet it is too often forgotten that a façade is after all part of the building, and not the least important. Shakespeare would not be the same to us if his name was Bacon, and that argument ought to suffice to stamp out the Baconian heresy. There is a massive majesty in *Milton* which is worthy of the poetry of *Paradise Lost.* Poets there are who were unlucky with their names, such as Corneille, yet there is a beauty, not wholly due to the poet's own greatness, in the adjective *cornélien.* Others, who improved on their lot with a sure instinct of what their name ought to be : thus Arouet, who admirably called himself Voltaire. There was a time when, owing to grave discrepancies between General and Madame Hugo, which very nearly led to a divorce, Victor Hugo was in danger of becoming Victor Trébuchet, a fact which would certainly have altered the nature of his poetry. Usually, however, French poets have been named by nature with true poetic insight. The names of Villon, Marot, Baudelaire, Leconte de Lisle, are true portraits of the poets who bore them. Nor is this matter of names to be dismissed as frivolous. There is little doubt that, absurd as it may seem, Nietzsche, an apostle of vigour and action, is often misunderstood as the very contrary owing to the associations which his name suggests with negative ideas such as *nirvana* and *nihilism.* Nowadays, Stravinsky has to contend not merely with long-acquired ear habits but with the suggestion of *extravagance* conveyed by his name. And who doubts but that Goethe has been helped both inwardly and outwardly in his ascent to the pinnacle of European literature by a name of such godlike majesty?

Don Ramón María del Valle Inclán is a poet with a good ear for the sounds and rhythms of the language. It is therefore meet that his name should naturally scan into a heroic if modern-moving hendecasyllabic. The line is indeed so perfect, and its qualities are so well balanced, that art could have found no better, and Nature, here represented by the poet's parents, reveals as delicate an insight into Castilian prosody as Don Ramón María del Valle Inclán himself, in the insertion of that admirable *María*, the graceful and feminine cadence of which lengthens the line to its heroic measure while it softens the somewhat too self-assertive succession of masculine accents in it. Rubén Darío, who knew a line of Castilian verse when he heard it, was so fascinated by this one that he made it the key-line of a famous ballad in praise of the poet whose name it sings. But its musical associations are not the only features which make this name so truly representative of our poet. There is also the sense of form which it reveals, a form neat and self-contained, though perhaps too exclusively based on the ear. And there is the knightly sonority of it all, which conveys a true suggestion of the nobiliary, rather than aristocratic, element in the poet's own poetry and fiction. There is that symbolic *María*, to remind us of the all-important place which woman occupies in his work. And there is lastly the bold defiance of such a high-sounding name amidst the drab restraint of the modern world, to suggest that Don Ramón María del Valle Inclán is not afraid of being thought strange and old-fashioned, nor even altogether above suspicion of a desire to *épater le bourgeois*.

Valle Inclán is, amongst contemporary Spanish poets, the most gifted in musical and formal powers.

The peculiar charm of his poetry is largely due to the interplay, and to a certain extent, the opposition, of two tendencies traceable to the two features of old Gallegan poetry : a popular vein, rich in emotion and rhythm, and a knowing taste for the formal refinements evolved by the exquisite genius of France. Our poet himself is not unaware of this double strain in his work, as shown by the following distich which he applies to his delicious *Marquesa Rosalinda*, but which can be said equally of all his poems :

> Olor de rosa y de manzana
> Tendrán mis versos a la vez.

> A scent of roses and of apples
> My verse will have at the same time.

It is the fresh country-like smell of apples which predominates in his *Aromas de Leyenda*. In this book of poems (1906), Galicia—a Galicia perhaps a little old-fashioned and beautified—is sung with its quiet hills, its wandering flocks and shepherds, its hermits and pilgrims, its grey atmosphere, which covers with a protective mantle dreams ever rising and never-dying beliefs. In this, his most truly poetical mood, Valle Inclán goes to the people for his inspiration. Every one of the poems of the book rises as it were from the contemplation of a popular song, in Gallegan, which is quoted at the end. No better summary could be given of that mood of restrained emotion, full of wisdom and experience, which our poet has known how to feel with the people and to render in his poetry, than this little popular jewel which is the kernel of one of his poems :

> Fuxe, meu meniño,   Fly, my little one,
> Que vou a chorar.   For now, I must weep.
> Séntate n'a porta,   Go, sit at the door,
> A ver choviscar.   And see the rain fall.

Together with this human emotion which he finds in

the earth of his native land, our poet reveals in these poems his delicate sensibility for the perception of the most elusive aspects of nature and an exceptional power of rendering them without apparent effort, as if by the simplest possible device. This device is indeed quite simple. It consists in giving to each word its full poetic power :

> Húmeda de la aurora, despierta la campana . . .
>
> Damp with the dawn, the bell awakes . . .

but that cannot be done unless the things themselves which the words represent have impressed on the poet's soul all the poetic power which they possess. And it is here, in his capacity for poetical impression, that this Gallegan poet probably surpasses every poet that ever wrote Castilian since Garcilaso. In him, the Genius of Water, which holds sway over his native land, has softened, without altogether abating, the Genius of Fire, which is, with the Genius of Air, the inspirer of true Castilian poetry, and thus he is the Spanish poet most capable of rendering nature with that touch of almost caressing love which is the main charm of Garcilaso's verse.

He resembles Garcilaso also in his capacity for assimilating foreign refinement. It is not Italy, nowadays, but France, which leads the evolution of poetical forms. Valle Inclán knows all the professional secrets of the art of Gautier and Banville, of Baudelaire and Verlaine, of Régnier and Viellé-Griffin. And yet it can hardly be said that he has studied them. The graces of French art seem to flourish naturally in this poet endowed by his race with just the right amount of sensibility to stir the Muse without breaking the well-balanced rhythm of her gait. It is this measure in emotion (which reminds us that *Gallegan* and *Gallic* have the same root) that makes our poet, though Spanish in temperament and vision, French in taste and in form. His emotion, even though genuine, is easily mastered, and as it were projected outwards into the world whence it came. The poet knows how to place himself at the right distance for the fashioning of his impression into a work of art. Valle Inclán is in fact that *rara avis* in Spanish letters : an artist.

The masterpiece of his courtly ' French ' style, is his *Marquesa Rosalinda*. This little poetical comedy is a unique gem in Castilian poetry. It proves in most brilliant fashion that that masculine language which seems fit only for the forcible accents of the epic ballad, the intense lyricism of the mystics, the grandiloquence of the conventional ode and the metallic blasts of warlike songs, can be rendered as slim and graceful as a Versailles *marquise*, as subtle as an eighteenth-century *abbé*, as nonchalant as a Verlainian decadent, as exquisitely humorous as a musical comedy of Mozart. The plot is conceived and developed in that half-serious, half-jesting mood which is the real mood of true comedy, so easy, yet so difficult to attain. It is admirably conveyed in these two lines which Rosa-linda sighs through her smiles as she sits down under a bower in her garden :

¡ Para llorar penas, qué lindo retiro !
¡ Lo menos tres ecos tiene aquí un suspiro !

For weeping one's sorrows, what a charming retreat !
Each sigh must have here three echoes at least !

This playful mood, not entirely frivolous but nearly so, delicately intellectual though not devoid of feeling, is more complex, more *precious* than is usual in Spanish literature. Both its earnestness and its stolidity prevent the Spanish genius from yielding such flowers, which Valle Inclán rightly calls ' rosas de Galia '. Indeed, the play seems French-inspired in more ways than one. There are here and there touches which suggest the direct influence of Rostand. Its *spadassins* seem skilful adaptations of that delicious bravo in *Les Romanesques*, who, hired to fight and simulate a defeat, presents his bill :

Habit froissé : vingt francs ; amour propre : quarante.

But this influence of Rostand only acts on the Spanish poet as a stimulus to his playful tendency. Nature and temperament are too deeply Spanish in him to allow his poetry to degenerate into a mere spinning of rhymed puns. The popular element, never wholly absent in him, even though it may be relegated to playing second fiddle, gives consistency, a body, to his most artificial-looking work. And thus there is throughout this comedy a curious Spanish essence not only unabsorbed by the French graces which adorn it, but even antagonistic to certain aspects of the French genius. In certain essential elements of his plot—the character of Rosalinda, for instance—as well as in some details of the dialogue—for example, the gibes at the French marquis—the play is almost aggressively Spanish. In its rhythmical grace *La Marquesa Rosalinda* is without rival in the language. Every scene is sung in its right melody, every line rings true, every word weds sound and sense in most felicitous harmony. An exquisite example of this musical perfection occurs in the Prelude—itself a delightful poem. It is a quatrain, already quoted, which sings and dances what its own words express :

Como en la gaita del galáico
Pastor, de la orilla del Miño,
Salte la gracia del trocáico
Verso, ligero como un niño.

As in the bagpipe of the Gallegan
Shepherd, by the banks of the Miño,
Let leap the grace of the trochaic
Verse, with the lightness of children.

Yet all is not Gallegan—whether rustic or courtly—in Valle Inclán. This name itself is too much in a major key to let us forget the heroic strain in the poetry which makes it illustrious. The poet who sang a pastoral rhapsody in his *Aromas de Leyenda*, who told a courtly and witty tale in his *Marquesa Rosalinda*, has proved that his voice can rise to the epic tone in a dramatic poem of great beauty : *Voces de Gesta* (1912). It is a poem, modern in the polish of its form, in the impeccable use of language and style, in the deliberate play of its effects, and in the skilful resources of its orchestration ; but old in its primitive vision of the human soul, with its virtues still fresh in the light of man's morning and its passions still roaming free like wolves in the unexplored forests of new lands. This contrast between a tempestuous, primeval nature and the refined art which reflects it like an impassive, limpid glass, might have given to *Voces de Gesta* the cold perfection of Parnassian poetry, were it not, again, for the popular element which restores to it the humility, the movement, and the warmth of life.

Now the epic-dramatic genius is not typically Gallegan, but Castilian. Don Ramón María del Valle Inclán is thus a Gallegan assimilated by Castile. He brings to Castilian poetry the distinctive lyrical gift of his land, but the strong dramatic power of the Centre finds in him so quick a response that he becomes one of its most inspired exponents. Nor is it possible to consider *Voces de Gesta* as a mere incursion into a kind of poetry foreign to his usual bent. Far from it. Drama is an inherent and most important element in his genius, so much so that it is perhaps by the consideration of this side of his art that his literary personality can be best understood.

The three elements of the poetry of Valle Inclán—

the lyrical-popular, the lyrical-courtly, and the epic-dramatic—reappear in his fiction. It is indeed doubtful whether a decision between poetry and fiction is possible in a work which is so imaginative in its poetical forms and so poetical in its novels. Our poet will have nothing to do with the humdrum world in which we all live. In the same haughty manner in which he passes through our modern matter-of-fact streets, his empty sleeve—for he is one-armed like Cervantes—dangling by his side, an old-world figure, with his long grey monkish beard, his tortoise-shell spectacles and his ascetic, receding forehead, so he presents to the noisy and busy multitudes that struggle for comfort and thirst for justice and truth, an art indifferent to modern ideals and devoted to the glorification of the passions.

> Había sonado para mí la hora en que se apagan los ardores de la sangre, y en que las pasiones del amor, del orgullo y de la cólera, las pasiones nobles y sagradas que animaron a los dioses antiguos, se hacen esclavas de la razón.[1]

So speaks in his winter mood his hero the Marquis of Bradomín. For this melancholy Don Juan, like the poet who created him, contemplates man in a purely æsthetic attitude and admires the passions for their inherent beauty as forces of nature manifesting their prime vigour in that most noble of creatures, man. His point of view is not that of the dealer in horses, who naturally prefers them to be tame, since it is tame they are useful, but that of the sculptor who enjoys the sight of them when wild and ungovernable. He therefore recoils instinctively from the city, with its well-thought-out system of laws which impose upon every man a certain minimum of virtue and

---

[1] For me the hour had come in which the ardour of the blood dies out, when the passions of love, of pride, and of anger, the noble and sacred passions which stirred the ancient gods, become the slaves of reason (*Sonata de Invierno*).

curb the passions under the weight of municipal regulations. His inspiration is kindled in those corners of Spain where there still lingers—or lingered when he wrote, for such things nowadays die out quickly—a life ruled by the primitive traditions of peasantry and chivalry : below, humility towards the lords of the land, stretching from heroic devotion to abject servility ; above, a natural authority founded on courage and high traditions, an egotism degenerating towards licence and tyranny ; and over all, high and low, the deeply rooted beliefs of a devotional religion enfolded in clouds of superstition, yet able to put the light of a meaning and the warmth of a hope into the most miserable life.

It is this primitive world in which the passions grow richer and purer than in our urban civilizations, where, like the trees of our cities, our passions are lightless and cheerless and covered with the grime and ashes of our hearths, it is this primitive world that Valle Inclán describes in his fiction. One of the three elements of his art will be found to predominate in each of the three groups into which his novels naturally fall. The first, the model of which is *Flor de Santidad,* is inspired by the peasant-like and religious lyricism of *Aromas de Leyenda.* The second, which is best represented by his four *Sonatas,* is the prose parallel to the courtly lyricism of *La Marquesa Rosalinda.* The epic-dramatic strain is most powerfully rendered in his two *Comedias Bárbaras,* i.e. *Aguila de Blasón* and *Romance de Lobos.*

Flor de Santidad is a picture of peasant life in Galicia, conceived in a distinctly poetical mood. The passions described are the elementary passions which animate primitive man : avarice and charity, ferocity and kindness, self-denial and lust, all moving freely and darkly in an atmosphere of superstition. The central figure is an orphan shepherdess who gives herself to a passing pilgrim believing him to be an incarnation of Jesus Christ. It is a story told with that skill for emotional music which is the secret of our poet-novelist, simple and humble in its subject-matter like a village tale, yet on a level higher than the mere matter-of-fact narrative of events. The typical features of the Gallegan genius are to be observed in it—the musical sense, the predominance of women and their point of view, and that peculiar atmosphere of commonalty in mansion, kitchen, and road which makes Galicia so murmuring and social. Yet the tale leaves an unpleasant impression, as if the author had not been fair to the poor folk whose superstition he exhibits. Had we felt that he shared the limitations of his characters, the story would have been more moving; had he written from the outside of them, it would have been more convincing. As it is, the impression that remains is one of insincerity.

It is also the impression left after reading the four exquisitely written sonatas. Here, the sense of music and form prevails to the point of imposing the name and method on the work. These four sonatas, one for each season of the year, correspond to four moments in the life of Xavier de Bradomín, a kind of melancholy and decadent Don Juan, who in his old age writes his memoirs so that the world may know of his love-triumphs before he repents. The character of Don Juan is one which fascinates Valle Inclán. It is in fact almost the only masculine character which he has really worked out in his prose and verse. The explanation is simple, and springs from that other feature which we have observed in Gallegan poetry, the predominance of women and their point of view. Don Juan is the only man compatible with this feature, since he is himself obsessed by women and of women he has the central tendency, namely, that which makes love the most important affair of life. Don

Juan, fundamentally, is a feminine character, and the
Don Juan of the four sonatas is a typically feminine
Don Juan. Which is far from meaning that he is
effeminate. The author finds him in that old-fashioned
Spanish aristocracy which in the second half of the
nineteenth century let itself go slowly down the slope
of decline in its old country seats, taking now and then
a half-hearted interest in the Carlist cause. With his
unfailing instinct for words, the poet novelist avoids
the traditional name for his Don Juan, and calls him
Xavier de Bradomín—a Christian name delicately
suggestive of an æsthetic, intellectual, decadent
Catholicism ; and a name, Gallegan in its cadence,
yet linked up by a vague verbal reminiscence with
gallant Brantôme. As for the hero's portrait, it is
brushed in three words : ' Era feo, católico y sentimental '. ' He was ugly, a Catholic, and sentimental.'
Very sentimental. Which means that he talks
about feeling more than he feels. Yet it must be
owned that he talks well, having at his disposal all
the resources of his creator's art. The four sonatas
are impeccable exercises of style, not of the burnished
style, relentlessly accurate, wherewith Flaubert can
raise headaches of a purely æsthetic origin, but rather
of that perfectly fluid form which flows in rhythm
with the emotions and faithfully reflects them. They
are four songs of love. It is not, however, Xavier,
the beloved, who gives them their emotional wealth,
but the women whom he fascinated throughout his
adventurous life. These women are admirably though
lightly and delicately rendered by an observer who
was admitted into the inmost chambers of their hearts
yet who could keep cool enough to note love's movements. In the sonatas, all the women are in earnest,
but the man they all love is not. Xavier is rather in
that half earnest, half frivolous mood which inspired *La
Marquesa Rosalinda*, only here the frivolous lies deeper

down, hidden under a pool of sentiment, and loses in grace and attractiveness by being cut off from the fresh air of sincerity. There is a sceptical undercurrent in Xavier's character which makes his melancholy melodies sound false and deceiving. We feel that a frank cynicism would have been pleasantly honourable by the side of this sentimental cant ! For this Don Juan, who goes about the world fascinating women, is not only incapable of repaying their love with love, however passing, but lives so low as not to be able to respect those souls who open themselves out to him. He lies to them as to facts, but that may be forgiven him, since lying of that sort is indispensable to a Don Juan—and herein a confirmation of the feminine character of the type. But, what is worse, he lies to them in spirit. He plays with them in a manner which is always unpleasant and sometimes repulsive. This feature gradually grows upon the reader until it destroys the implicit nobility of the character. The manly animal qualities of aristocracy— courage, pride, and a kind of natural authority—are his and well rendered. But his generosity is external and showy ; his loyalty for his king, the whim of a decadent dilettante : his sensibility, never higher than curiosity stimulated by lust ; of religion he knows nothing but its picturesque side ; and thus the type which the author meant to be noble has no real nobility in his heart.

Our poet-novelist has brushed a rougher, ruder, and altogether greater type of Spanish nobleman in his Don Juan Manuel Montenegro, the hero of his *Comedias Bárbaras*. The *Comedias Bárbaras* are two novels written in dialogue. The first of these stories— *Aguila de Blasón*—may be considered as a first attempt at what the author achieves in the second. *Romance de Lobos* is a masterpiece of dramatic vigour and concentration. It has all the violent quality of an etching by Goya. Don Juan Montenegro is a magnificent human beast, a kind of centaur of the passions—the noble as well as the low ones—a tyrant both loved and feared by the peasantry, who lets his fortune slowly go in grants to avaricious but complaisant husbands and fathers on his estates. The drama derives its barbaric strength from the opposition between his overpowering will and the brutal behaviour of his five sons, the heirs of all his unruly passions but not of his noble traditions. The central fact is the death of *Dama Maria*, the nobleman's long-suffering wife, the desolate mother of the five ferocious brigands. The vision which overtakes Don Juan Manuel when, riding back drunk from the fair, he falls from his horse in the night; his crossing in the stormy night, after over-ruling by his spirit and contemptuous taunts the wise fears of the mariners; his meeting in the night with a band of beggars whom he leads to his house for a distribution of alms in alleviation of his sins; the sack of the mansion by the five heartless brigands while their mother lies on her death-bed; the fight between Don Juan Manuel and his eldest son, inter-rupted by a gigantic leper, the leader of the beggars, whose fearless religious majesty forces the young brigand to stay his hand raised against his father; the despair of Don Juan Manuel at the sight of his dead wife; his public confession; then that wonderful final scene at the gates of the palace, now in the hands of the five, when the old homeless nobleman at the head of the band of beggars knocks; the door that opens, the old man who advances, the beggars who hesitate, then, boldly led by the leper, go forward; then the fight, the young brigand attacking a beggar, the old man that slaps his face, the brigand that drives his fist in his father's venerable face, and the leper coming forward and knocking the heartless brigand down amidst the shouts of the beggar crowd, all these

scenes are made alive with such generous inspiration
that the very language sings like a harp in the winds
of the storm and, without conscious effort, the
dramatic mood becomes lyrical.

The closing scene in particular gives to the drama
an earnestness and a gravity which saves it from mere
picturesqueness. For the figure of Don Juan Manuel,
like that of his five sons, suffers from the defect of its
qualities. It is too simple in its romantic freedom
from all restraint. It lacks subtlety. It is precisely
this lack of subtlety in his characters which makes
Aguila de Blasón, despite its vigour and the dramatic
quality of its plot, somewhat unsatisfactory. In
Romance de Lobos, however, that popular element
which often comes to the rescue of our novelist when
his fancy threatens to run away with his common sense,
stands him in good stead, and for once also his religion,
which is too often but a pretext for pretty sights and
quaint feelings, becomes earnest and purposeful, and
Don Juan Manuel is at last sincere and is at last a man.
Yet, here and there, even in *Romance de Lobos*, we hear
the jarring note of insincerity. It may be a metaphor
a little self-conscious, it may be a bombastic phrase or
an overstrained feeling, which appears as soon as
the fury of action abates and the narrator can hear
himself speak and has time to think of what he is
doing. So that, even in this his masterpiece, Valle
Inclán does not allow us to forget that the metal of
his art is not so pure as its beautiful colour might
lead us to expect.

What is it then which makes this art, exquisite and
vigorous as it is, somewhat ineffective ? Why does it
not live within us like Hamlet or Don Quixote, but
remains outside, on the mantlepiece or on the table,
like a chiselled snuff-box ? We have observed that it
is seldom in earnest. Once, in *La Marquesa Rosalinda*,

this lack of earnestness is, through sheer art, turned into a delight. But then it is the world of comedy, and the earnestness of a certain type of comedy consists precisely in not being earnest. Once again, through sheer epic imagination, this art attains a great level and closes *Romance de Lobos* with a scene which deserves to live. But for the rest, while acknowledging that the artist sings well and paints admirably, we feel that his art sounds hollow. Why?

Whenever the work of an artist appears to suffer from one dominant defect, it is wise to search for the root of this defect in the very region where the root of his main quality lies. The main quality of Valle Inclán, that which gives formal excellence and emotional music to his art, is the purity of his æsthetic attitude. He turns his soul on nature like a mirror, the limpidity of which is untarnished by any moral or philosophical preoccupation. He sees, feels, and reflects in perfect peace. Now, this is as it should be. A work of art should be—indeed, can only be—conceived in a purely æsthetic attitude, which neither the eagerness to learn nor the desire to teach should disturb. Neither proving nor improving have anything to do with art.

But when we have said that the mood in which the artist looks at life should be free from ethical or philosophical influences, we do not mean that the artist himself should be altogether free from ethical and philosophic preoccupations. Here lies the kernel of that most vexing question, art for art's sake. Yes, of course, art must be for art's sake. But provided the artist has a philosophic mind and an ethical heart. Let his mood, while creating, be wholly æsthetic, but not the soul which goes into that mood. Ethics and philosophy are not the music of art, but they are the sounding-box which gives depth and sonority to it. Let the artist look at Life with purely æsthetic eyes, but unless his mind breathe the high summits of thought and his soul move true to his divine origin, his art will never rise above that of the embroiderer—and it will never grow.

It is here, to my mind, that the flaw in the art of Don Ramón María del Valle Inclán is to be found. His æsthetic attitude is not merely the natural one of an artist intent on creation. It arises also from a real indifference towards the higher philosophic and moral issues. His emotion is purely æsthetic, and evokes no resonances in the recesses of his soul. The vacuum which surrounds the strings of his sensibility reflects back its inaneness on the sound that they yield. The æsthetic emotion itself, lacking the necessary resonance, becomes thin and false. Hence that jarring note of insincerity throughout his work. There is in it a literary preoccupation which savours too much of the *métier*. It comes out now and then in the use of bookish expressions, such as ' celtic stones ', or the word ' classic ' in the following lines from *Romance de Lobos*, referring to the complexion of an old woman :

> . . . con ese color oscuro y clásico que tienen las nueces de los nogales centenarios. . . .
> . . . with that dark and classic colour of the nuts of centenary walnut-trees. . . .

It explains the indifference with which man's most sacred passions are handled without leaving the slightest tremor in the hands of the artist, a circumstance which leads him to commit strange breaches of taste.[1] It stimulates the search for the merely weird

---

[1] Thus the episode with Isabel in *Sonata de Otoño*. Concha, one of his mistresses, has called Xavier to her house, for she is dying. After a few days of joy, she sinks fast, and dies late at night, in his arms, in his bed, far from her bedroom. Xavier roams through the palace, seeking the help of Isabel, his cousin, in order to remove the body to the dead woman's room and so avoid a scandal. He knocks at Isabel's door, but she is asleep. He enters and touches her bare arm. She

and picturesque, for the horrible and the morbid. It is, in fine, the manifestation of an æsthetic sensibility without philosophical guidance nor ethical ballast.

Nor is this meant to imply that Valle Inclán is lacking in mental powers and curiosity. Far from it. His work is full of most ingenious symbols, images, and ideas which reveal a penetrating mind. It is not from lack of ideas that his work suffers, nor do we here suggest that it is worthless because of its unmoral philosophy. This philosophy, which is that of the freedom of passion as opposed to the philosophy of repression and discipline, is perfectly defensible, and the deliberate choice of it implies in Valle Inclán a power for discernment and a capacity for high thought which no one thinks of denying him. He fails, not because he lacks a philosophy, nor because his philosophy is wrong, but because, once he has adopted it, he does not succeed in convincing us that he really believes in it inherently. Rather does he convey the impression that his choice is purely determined by the æsthetic advantages which he detects in the point of view which he adopts. And this impression is sufficient to sap the vitality of his æsthetic emotion itself.

Frivolity is thus the sterile wasp which eats the heart of that beautiful *rosa de Galia* grown in Gallegan soil by Don Ramón María del Valle Inclán. And this is the secret why the rose does not grow, but, slowly paler and paler, drops now and then a petal, always fine, always scented with exquisite perfume, always frail and thin, and ever the same.

awakes, and being, of course, in love with him, mistakes the situation. Xavier there and then forgets his dead mistress, and makes the most of the mistake.

AZORÍN[1]

GABRIEL MIRÓ

SEEN in its entirety, above the historical and political contingencies which have obscured its intrinsic unity, the Spanish Peninsula appears as one well-defined spiritual entity. This fact the Portuguese critics are beginning to realize and the Catalan critics to forget. Both movements are historically logical, for, while Portugal has outlived the period of her affirmation as a separate sub-entity within the Spanish wider unity, Catalonia is on the contrary but beginning a struggle for asserting her own personality within the Peninsula and putting it beyond reach of attack from political prejudice. Strife psychology is never the ideal atmosphere for thought, and so it will be found that Catalan critics do not always realize the true strength of the ties which bind them to the Peninsula, nay, of the roots which make them part and essence of the spirit of the Peninsula as the land they inhabit is part of its body. But the spiritual unity of Spain [2] does not depend on the vagaries of critics, being grounded on deeper realities. Yet these vagaries do serve a useful purpose, since they bring into relief a fact no less important than that which they tend to obscure, namely, that Spain is not a simple, but a complex unity, a trinity composed of a Western, a Central, and an Eastern modality, the norms of which respectively are Portugal, Castile, and Catalonia. Three languages (or groups of languages) embody

[1] A pseudonym. His real name is José Martínez Ruiz.
[2] Spain is the real name of the whole Peninsula, and includes Portugal as well as Catalonia. It is a more exact word than Iberia, if only because the adjective Iberian is vague and belongs to anthropology rather than to history and literature.

these three spiritual modalities of the Spanish race. In the West, the Atlantic modality finds its expression in the Portuguese, of Latin languages the most tender and melodious. In the Centre, the Continental modality inspires that stately Castilian in which strength and grace are as harmoniously combined as tragedy and comedy in good drama. To the East, the Mediterranean modality shapes Catalan and its dialects, languages as supple and soft as clay, as vivid as painters' palettes, as receptive as the still waters of the clean sea which bathes the shores where they are spoken.

In literature and the arts the character of each of these three modalities of Spain may be defined by the predominance of one particular æsthetic tendency. This predominant or specific tendency is in the West lyrical, epic-dramatic in the Centre, and plastic in the East. The lyrical attitude is personal and has for its object the artist himself. The artist sees life as a flow and listens to the murmurs which rise as this flow falls on his own soul. The dramatic attitude is passive and has for its object the world of men. The artist conceives life as an endless drama between character and destiny. The plastic tendency is active. The hand stretches towards matter, eager to impress upon it the form obscurely felt in the artist's soul. Matter is therefore the object of the plastic creator, and his way of approach is through the outer crust towards the inner meaning of things. Thus we find in the Eastern modality of the Spanish race the qualities and the defects of the plastic tendency. The Catalan possesses a firm hold on the material aspects of things and a determination to stamp his own personality on the clay of life which can be felt, for instance, in certain cadences of his language. Let the sounds be compared of the words *génie* and *seny*,[1] and the difference will be perceived

[1] Pronounce *seyn*.

between a geometric line drawn on a white paper by a mathematician and the heavy impress of a sculptor's thumb on a piece of soft clay. There is always in the Catalan an implicit form which demands as its right some matter in which to become embodied, thus passing from mind into space. Hence a certain sense of order which has misled some people, amongst them many Catalans, into believing Catalonia to be a kind of French spiritual *enclave* in Spain. But the French sense of order is the outcome of a logical type of mind, while the Catalan sense of order is due to a plastic feeling. The French sense of order can be put on paper, is successive and has but two dimensions, and is felt instantaneously, while the Catalan sense of order is three-dimensional, like the feelings of up and down, back and front, top, middle, and base, symmetry, and, most mysterious of all, the feeling that guides the arrangement of useless objects on a mantelpiece.

Yet this feeling of order, though plastic and not logical, does give Catalonia the position of a *liaison* country between Europe and the rest of Spain. Europe, that is the West-Central-European nucleus which more consciously and intelligently represents the ideals of the white race, has chosen the Apollinian rather than the Dionysian path for its way up to the Temple of Mysteries, and, though careful not to reject Dionysian testimonies, yet looks on them with Apollinian eyes. Both the Western and Central types of the Spanish genius partake of the Dionysian rather than of the Apollinian nature. Not so Catalonia. If not always in actual life, at least in her ideals, she is Greek ; Greek in that ' classic ' sense which corresponds to a literary rather than to a truly historical view of the Hellenic nature, Greek not as Aeschylus but as Goethe. The most original and vigorous of modern Catalan minds, Eugenio d'Ors, has expressed this ideal in a striking little passage :

It is impossible to speak about Goethe coolly. We are troubled by something which it is difficult to confess, yet impossible to disown. We are troubled by *envy*.

The worst kind of envy, for it does not aim at attributes, but at the substance. Usually we envy great figures some one of their properties or qualities. We should like to possess their eminent gift or their priceless booty, but without ceasing to be ourselves. . . . But our passion towards Goethe is more grave, for it tempts us to the blasphemy of renouncing our own personality.

We should like to *speak* like Demosthenes, to *write* like Boccaccio, to *know* as much as Leibniz, to *possess*, like Napoleon, a vast empire, or, like Ruelbeck, a Botanic Garden. . . . We should like to *be* Goethe.

All Olympian souls see in this Olympian the image of their own selves elevated to its maximum power, glory and serenity.

Here, the Central European ideal of Catalonia is asserted with all the ingenuity and, be it noted, the ' three-dimensional ' precision of the Catalan plastic mind. This choice of Goethe as a model is typical, For neither Castile nor Portugal could ever consider Goethe as their ideal. Rather would they turn to Shakespeare, despite his lack of ' Olympian ' manners. And the reasons is that while Western and Central Spain aim at character, Catalonia aims at culture.

Catalonia is determined to plod on the road of progress. Leaving the contemplation of Eternity to the Castilian, she is well content with Time, and particularly with the present time as manifest in the sundry objects of everyday life. The Mediterranean Spaniard is no ascetic. He feels the *joie de vivre* and lives. He does not seek the high summits of speculation, and finds enough grounds for intellectual enjoyment in the many sights of the valley below. He approaches these sights precisely as sights, not as symbols of some higher or deeper significance but merely as objects the shape and colour of which are in themselves a sufficient attraction. The Catalan is sensuous.

A Spaniard he still is in that his nature is synthetic rather than analytic. But he differs from the two other types in that he develops along the line of talent and intellect rather than along that of genius and spirit. Thus Catalonia is—mentally—a land of plains at a good medium level, below which and above which fall and rise the inequalities of Castilian genius. The Catalan talent is hard-working and purposeful. It knows the use of the file and of that literary instrument which Flaubert called *gueuloir*. Spanish still in that it improvises, it is no longer so in that it tries to refine the material thrown up by improvisation—a sculptor endeavouring to chisel Greek statuettes in lava.

As it moves south, the Catalan genius, without losing its main plastic tendency, changes considerably in every other respect. Valencia is a land of flame and colour, painted in vivid tones—the gold and green of its orange-groves, the ochre of its earth, the pale blue of its skies, the dazzling white of its low houses over which now and then towers an eastern-looking cupola covered with dark-blue glazed tiles. Here beauty is so abundant on the surface of the world that men forget how to seek for it below. Any one is an artist, any thing a work of art. Thus Valencia disperses its genius and gains in surface what it loses in depth. It is a land of painters, with a decorative talent and a fine feeling for the values of light and quality over the surface of things. When power is added, work of great descriptive value may result. Thus, Blasco Ibáñez.

There is to the south of Valencia a land historically within the kingdom,[1] but spiritually a thing apart. It is the province of Alicante. North of it stretch the colour and flame of Valencia proper; east, the

---

[1] The town of Valencia is the capital of the Kingdom of Valencia.

Latin sea ; north-west, La Mancha, the very lands in which Don Quixote was born.   Just as Galicia is the transition between lyrical Portugal and dramatic Castile, so Alicante is the transition between dramatic Castile and the plastic East.   Here, the spirit of the Centre touches the spirit of the East, Castile looks on the Mediterranean.   The dramatic feeling of man emerges from its depths of concentration and meets on the surface the plastic sense of things.   This delicately poised zone of the Spanish spirit is represented in Spanish letters by two contemporary authors : Azorín and Gabriel Miró.

Both these authors are East-Spaniards in their plastic outlook.   Both look at life with the eyes of painters ; not of painters like the Grecos of old and the Zuloagas of our day, who allow their inner ghost to guide their brush away from the primary aspects of reality, but of accurate and faithful observers of the surface of things. In both of them, we are struck by the vigour of that feeling for matter which is the typical feature of plastic Spain as of all plastic characters.   Colour, texture, sound, inclination, reverberation, all effects on eyes, ears, skin, are most minutely observed, most felicitously rendered by both.   A cursory glance at a garden and Azorín will note : ' the light green of the orange trees and the dark green of the pomegranates '.[1] And Miró, while relating a casual conversation, will seize and express this most trivial detail with exquisite accuracy : ' Don Magín lighted a cigarette and, his palate covered with a wool of smoke which made his voice sound graver, proceeded. . . .' [2]   This pictorial

[1] El verde claro de los naranjos y el verde oscuro de los granados (Azorín, *Los Pueblos*, p. 19).
[2] Encendió Don Magín un cigarrillo y con el paladar empañado y la voz gruesa de vellones de humo, proseguía (G. Miró, *Nuestro Padre San Daniel*).

character of their art is emphasized by the use of the present tense. Both Azorín and Miró evince a significant leaning towards putting their verbs in the present, a tense which is essentially pictorial and *presents* events as scenes before the reader's eyes. Their narrative work is thus generally composed of a series of pictures, not moving as in the theatre or the cinema, but passing one after the other before our eyes as in a picture gallery. These pictures are usually understood in the manner of brilliant sketches, accurate yet not photographic, for their accuracy is due to the skilful selection of important and telling details, their brilliance to the illumination of these details by a style always clear. Both seem to paint with a sunbeam for a brush.

And then, they are not mere painters. Both approach life from its surface, but have also a feeling for the world of spirit underneath, a kind of uneasiness which does not allow them merely to rest on the surface and gives a human value, and incidentally distinction, to their pictorial work. In them the plastic movement from the surface inwards is met by a spiritual movement from the depths outwards, a kind of human emotion which reveals the Castilian element in their nature. And it is in the eddies of these two æsthetic waves meeting that their inspiration takes its rise. Hence, these two artists—for they are artists, being of the East—while loving the surface of things with the sensuous love of the plastic Spaniard, give to their treatment of it a tremulous quality which makes it alive and is to their art like the bloom of fresh-gathered fruit.

Of the two, Azorín is the better artist. His eyes wander nearer the surface of things. He is in reality a miniaturist. When he began to write, he made his person and style conspicuous by two affectations : he wore an eyeglass and he made a lavish use of the personal pronoun.[1] His style was made up of a series of short sentences, all beginning with I, *Yo*. The effect is as if this *Yo* was itself the eyeglass on Azorín's sharp, observant eye : the Y, the handle, the O, the set orb of the lens ; and the rest of the sentence, the little image, observed, all neat and searched in every detail, like the images reflected in the pupil. The freshness and luminosity of these images, the novelty of the technique, were the first qualities to be noted in the new-comer. And then it began to be realized that Azorín was deliberately selecting everyday objects with his eyeglass. His *Yo* was turned, not on romantic castles, lyrical gardens, and the heroes of the past, nor on great works, ships, seas, expanses of land and masses of people, and the deeds of modern men, but on chairs, tables, pots and pans, and a bit of garden which was not even solitary nor sad, but just as every garden usually is, and the men and women who while away their time in little towns of Spain where nothing happens but the hand of the sun caressing the idle walls of the gardens and the hand of the moon gliding over the sleeping roofs. And this keen observer went about and *saw.* He saw what had never been seen before, that all these familiar things inhabited by these familiar people, were really clad with beauty. All they wanted was an eye armed with a clear-sighted *Yo* like an eyeglass that would look at them. We may well apply to him what he himself said of Juan Luis Vives : He ' has felt probably better than any one else the eternal poetry of little everyday things '.[2]

He sees it, of course, because it is in him. But also

---

[1] The Spanish language has different forms for the several persons of the verb, and therefore personal pronouns are rarely used, except for purposes of emphasis.

[2] Juan Luis Vives ha sentido acaso mejor que nadie la eterna poesía de lo pequeño y cuotidiano (*Lecturas Españolas*).

because he knows how to look for it in the world outside. Azorín is a conscious artist. He has himself
informed us of his habit of noting down scenes and
pictures. 'How many little note-books did I fill with
notes once! *La Voluntad, Antonio Azorín, Los
Pueblos,* are written after the minute, accurate—I
believe accurate—notation in my little books.'[1]
Thus we see the raw material for his work patiently
gathered on the spot by an industrious hand. But,
though careful to note down the fleeting expression
on the face of nature at the moment when it occurs,
our artist is not content to use his notes as they stand.
We observe that he says his works were written ' after ',
not ' on ' his notes. For his style, though free and
graceful, is not spontaneous, and at moments we seem
to detect in its smooth surface the places in which
the file did work, but not enough.

The usual fault with such careful and conscious art
is that it is apt to leave an impression of coldness.
Not so with Azorín. For though he remains near the
surface of things, and in an attitude on the whole
plastic, he nevertheless penetrates into the spirit
below and never loses sight of the human. In his early
days, he manifested this human, dramatic, element of
his art by means of an artifice of style similar to his
use and abuse of the personal pronoun. It consisted
in the crowding of his pages with Christian names.
Instead of writing : ' Suddenly, several people entered
the room ', he would say : ' Suddenly I saw Don
Fernando and María and Isabel and Doña Clarita,
and Doña Remedios and Don Juan and Don José.'

---

[1] ¡Cuantos cuadernitos he llenado de notas antaño! ... *La Voluntad,
Antonio Azorín, Los Pueblos,* están escritos según la notación minu-
ciosa y exacta — creo que exacta — de mis cuadernitos. (Note in
Páginas Escogidas, published by Editorial Saturnino Calleja.) The
two first books mentioned are novels. The third a book of sketches
of Spanish life.

Azorín has outgrown this little trick of style as he has outgrown several other affectations, but the tendency which inspired it is inherent in his personality and can be seen in the dramatic vigour of some of his little pictures, such as that delightful sketch *Los Toros*, which is, and deserves to be, dedicated to Zuloaga.[1]

In fact, this kind of short, dramatic picture, blending the plastic and the dramatic elements in him, is the most typical work of Azorín. Such books as *Castilla*, *Los Pueblos*, are admirable little albums of Spanish life in which the reader is taken away from the beaten track, away also from exceptional and picturesque sights and incidents, and made to see, hear, taste, and enjoy the real commonplace Spain as it lives every day and everywhere—the whole through the sensibility of an exquisite artist endowed with a rare gift for atmosphere and detail.

This art is always very near the surface. Yet it is not shallow. For Azorín is served here by his excellent sense of proportion, and never writes at length. After all, shallowness and profundity are not absolute values, but mere relations between the depth and the other dimensions in the work of art. The depth of *As You Like It* would be shallow for *King Lear*, but is not so for *As You Like It*. This, Azorín has realized fully, and as he feels his art limited in depth he deliberately limits the length and the width of his little sketches to the proportions which will make satisfactory works of art. In this, his virtue, he finds himself helped by a certain natural shortness of breath which prevents him from attempting long literary exertions. This fact explains, in part at least, that both his novels and his criticism should resolve themselves into the same kind of literary sketches which are at bottom the only kind of work Azorín has produced.

[1] It will be found in *Los Pueblos*.

There are other reasons. As a novelist, Azorín has
not sufficient creative power to wander away from
direct observation. The surface of life which he can
watch with so much plastic love is animated to his
eyes by a human and vital emotion which makes it
vibrate. But, though penetrating enough to paint,
he is not penetrating enough to create, because he
needs the eyes of his body and matter to contemplate.
And then, there seems to be no real synthetic philosophy behind his sensibility. ' I will select '—he says
in one of his books—' I will select from among my
memories some notes as vivid and disconnected as
reality itself.' [1] It may seem at first sight unfair to
take a passing remark such as this as a basis for a literary
character. Yet, this saying is so much in keeping with
Azorín's general attitude towards life and letters that
it is difficult not to look upon it as the faithful expression of his considered thought. It reveals the precise
level from which Azorín the thinker looks upon life.
He is penetrating enough to see that life is vivid and
disconnected, yet not enough to realize that, below
this layer, life is again one ; and this insufficiency of
his synthetic outlook is reflected in his lack of creative
power.

A similar statement in another of his books places
him on exactly the same level as a critic.

There is, I believe, a distant connexion between the
personal nature of an author and his manner of writing.
There are passionate, impetuous men, who write in a quiet
and equable manner. There are men serene and easy-going
in private life, who, pen in hand, prove to be hot and
unbalanced writers.[2]

[1] Yo tomaré entre mis recuerdos algunas notas vivaces e inconexas —
como lo es la realidad (*Confesiones de un Pequeño Filósofo*).

[2] Hay una muy lejana relación — tal creemos — entre las con-
diciones personales del autor y su manera de escribir. Hombres
pasionales, impetuosos, escriben de un modo discreto y ecuánime.

Here, then, is a mind capable of observing the anomalies noted down in the second part of the sentence, yet not capable of avoiding the hopeless conclusion with which the statement opens. This quotation illustrates the psychological weakness which impairs the work of Azorín as a critic in the current and normal sense of the word. Whether as a novelist or as a critic, Azorín suffers from a lack of a synthetic philosophy worthy of his fine artistic powers.

Yet, neither his novels nor his criticism can be laid aside as worthless. Far from it. They are amongst the most precious of modern Spanish productions. Only they must be considered as mere varieties of Azorín's central work, the plastic interpretation of Spanish life. His novels are little series of pictures, ' vivid and disconnected ', and at most linked up by a more or less vague plot. As for his criticism, Azorín has turned his famous eye both on moderns and on classics, but with unequal fortune. Curiously enough, this plastic artist who requires the direct contemplation of his material to work at ease, is more successful with the old than with the new writers. The paradox is but apparent and solves itself easily enough. The moderns are not sufficiently ' set ' for the eye of the painter to see them. They are bad sitters. They will not keep quiet. While the old ones . . . Azorín has painted little dramatic sketches of them which make the venerable figures appear bright and human, as they spoke and dressed and ate and sat and walked and wore their hats, in the times when they were men and not mere names. And this *re-animation* of human beings whom heartless professors—spiritual vultures—had killed in order to prey on their remains—this re-creation of life, being the very definition of art, should be suffi-

Hombres serenos, placenteros, en la vida privada, son de un desquiciamiento ardoroso con la pluma en la mano (*Páginas Escogidas*. Preface).

cient to make his name endure in Spanish letters as
the artist who saw little but saw so well that wherever
his eye fell, there was life.

Gabriel Miró is nearer to the Castilian spirit than
Azorín. He certainly is an Easterner. His vision is full
of the light of the Mediterranean sea. ' In my town,'
he says himself, ' from the moment we are born, our
eyes are filled with the blueness of the waters.' [1]   And
this luminosity is still the prevailing quality of his art.
His approach to nature is still through the surface,
and his tendency is plastic, as if to seize and mould
what his senses, and particularly his eyes, perceive.
He has the powers of minute observation which go
with the plastic attitude, those powers which seem to
consist in a mere capacity for stating what is there,
before eyerybody's eyes, and yet are ever so much
deeper, rooted in the recesses of sensibility. He has
also, of the Easterner the deliberate attitude. He
looks in order to see. We miss with him that casual
air of the Castilian who seems to see without deliberately looking. Gabriel Miró is an active observer and
a conscious artist.

He is, however, as an artist, both inferior to and more
spontaneous than Azorín. The material in him is not
so finely worked out by the skilful plastic mind.
Now and then we feel an awkward sentence, a word
out of place, a turn of idiom which is not quite pleasing
or adequate. They are, to be sure, small faults, such
faults as we would never notice in other writers, but
which, here, leap to the eye, as scratches on the surface
of burnished gold. Moreover, the matter with which
Gabriel Miró deals is of a heavier, denser nature than
that of Azorín. While Azorín prefers to seek his
æsthetic emotion in the atmosphere which surrounds

---

[1] En mi ciudad, desde que nacemos, se nos llenan los ojos de azul de
las aguas (*El Ángel, El Molino, El Caracol del Faro*, p. 131).

the objects of his observation, Miró seems on the contrary to seek emotion in the springs of life that lie hidden within the objects themselves. A more solid mind, he gives things more solidity. A graver mind, he gives them more weight. Hence often the impression that the material which he shapes is more rebellious to the hand than the light and air with which Azorín paints his little pictures.

For Miró is more profoundly affected than Azorín by the spirit of Castile. His material is more densely laden, more intimately amalgamated with human substance. The reader is often arrested by striking images in which a purely plastic form appears filled with a sense which is almost immaterial.

> Silence flowed densely from their mouths as dumb water from a gloomy rock.[1]

Examples such as this could be found in practically every page of his works. They reveal a tendency to dwell in that zone of the mind where nature and man are seen, not exactly as one thing, but as two faces of one thing, so that our imagination naturally expresses the one in terms of the other. It is a region in which high poetry is conceived, and, given the power, created. Through his plastic road of access, Miró has penetrated farther than his countryman into the soul of poetry, for, though not so good an artist, he has a deeper sense of nature and man. Not that Azorín is lacking in this quality. He would not be an artist at all if he were. But while, in him, the poetical quality seems to be adjectival to his plastic tendency and merely to enhance and render more exquisite his pictorial ability, in Miró it is vital and strongly felt, it is in fact as central as his plastic tendency, and it sharpens and prolongs his penetration.

---

[1] . . . el silencio manaba densamente de sus bocas como el agua muda de una peña sombría (*Nuestro Padre San Daniel*, p. 174).

This poetic virtue is in Miró so natural and pure that he can, without effort, without almost meaning it, write limpid poetry in three or four simple words of prose that do not change the tone of the whole. Thus, speaking of a pool of clear water :

> And the foliage, the trunks, the rock, the cloud, the blue, the bird, all is seen within ; and many a time we know that all this is beautiful because the water says it.[1]

Because the water says it. This is more than mere simplicity. It is limpidity. And it is more than art. It is a clean spring of poetry born of a clear, luminous mind. The sentence which follows leads to a conclusion of no lesser beauty :

> Then, everything takes on the mystery and the life of its [the water's] emotion. It is now beauty contemplated ; it is now the conception and the formula of a beauty which is created in that solitude as in the soul of man, and the water is like a forehead which has thought this landscape.[2]

We feel here the superiority of Miró over Azorín. His mind is deeper and more capable of a synthetic emotion of the world. This reveals itself primarily in superior powers of creation. I believe that Miró has been misled by his sheer plastic imagination into writing his two volumes of *Figuras de la Pasión*. They no doubt represent a fine effort to re-create several episodes directly or indirectly connected with the life and death of Christ. Often, as in his episode of Herodes Antipas, the ingenious turn given to the story adds a special merit of its own to what would otherwise have been a mere historical *pastiche*. But

---

[1] Y los follajes, los troncos, la peña, la nube, el azul, el ave, todo se ve dentro, y, muchas veces, se sabe que es hermoso porque el agua lo dice (*El Ángel, El Molino, El Caracol del Faro*, p. 110.)

[1] Entonces, todo adquiere el misterio y la vida de la emoción suya. Es ya la belleza contemplada ; es el concepto y la fórmula de una belleza que se produce en esa soledad como en el alma del hombre, y el agua es como una frente que ha pensado este paisaje.

the style, in its effort to render the splendour of Jewish, Roman, and Assyrian life, is apt to take on that hard-driven gait which makes *Salammbô* such a painful book to read. Certainly, admirers of Flaubert's plastic efforts should find themselves at home in Miró's *Figuras de la Pasión*. But the true business of a Spanish artist is to make poetry with the here and now. And it is in this work that the best of Miró must be looked for. He has written several novels and books of sketches. The best—a good sign—are the latest. Many a fine page may be found in his *El Humo Dormido*, reminiscences of childhood written in a manner not unlike that of Marcel Proust, though fortunately with a more adequate idea of the right proportions between length and depth as well as of the time available for reading in the modern world. In *Nuestro Padre San Daniel*, ' a novel of chaplains and devout people ', Miró has written a work which reveals the earnestness of his human preoccupation. There is in him an undercurrent of tenderness which gives his work a slightly melancholy tone. He is never rancorous, like Baroja, nor an ethical dilettante, like Valle Inclán, nor depressing like—but Spaniards are never depressing. He is just a little sad, as if he deplored that nature could be so beautiful and yet men so unworthy of it. Then, on the brink of coming to this conclusion, he repents. This attitude is admirably expressed in one of the most interesting stories in his best book.[1] It is a story of an angel who settles down on Earth. A cherub comes to fetch him back. His wings have fallen, he has grown a beard and has become used to the ways of men. He gives the cherub a most pessimistic view of man's nature. The cherub then says : ' Well, I came to fetch you. Rise and come up.' But the angel says ' No '. And the exquisite page in

---

[1] *El Ángel, El Molino, El Caracol del Faro.*

which he explains why he wants to stay on earth can be summed up in this line of his, which is perhaps the kernel of Miró's philosophy : 'How sweet it is to feel near Heaven on Earth ! ' [1]

This little book is full of such jewels, written with an eye that searches nature to its minutest details, but also with such an intensity of human feeling that we hardly know where man ends and nature begins in the delicate blend. The danger of such an art is that it may—it sometimes does—degenerate into fancy. As a rule, however, it is the creation of a bright, pene-trating, and sensitive imagination, sustained by a poetic feeling of such simplicity and truth that it can elevate the statement of commonplaces to heights of limpid beauty as in this sentence, the serenity of which must not be troubled by translation : 'El alma del agua sólo reside en la tranquila plenitud de su origen.'

[1] ¡ Qué dulce es sentirnos cerca del cielo desde la tierra !

Printed in England at the Oxford University Press